Bismarck – the Epic Sea Chase

Bismarck –
the Epic Sea Chase

by

Jim Crossley

Pen & Sword
MARITIME

First published in Great Britain in 2010 by
Pen & Sword Maritime
an imprint of
Pen & Sword Books Ltd
47 Church Street
Barnsley
South Yorkshire
S70 2AS

Copyright © Jim Crossley 2010

ISBN: 978-1-84884-250-2

The right of Jim Crossley to be identified as Author of this Work
has been asserted by him in accordance with the Copyright, Designs
and Patents Act 1988.

A CIP catalogue record for this book is
available from the British Library.

Typeset in 11/13pt Palatino by
Concept, Huddersfield, West Yorkshire

Printed and bound in England by
the MPG Books Group

Pen & Sword Books Ltd incorporates the Imprints of Pen & Sword
Aviation, Pen & Sword Maritime, Pen & Sword Military, Wharncliffe
Local History, Pen & Sword Select, Pen & Sword Military Classics,
Leo Cooper, Remember When, Seaforth Publishing and
Frontline Publishing.

For a complete list of Pen & Sword titles please contact
PEN & SWORD BOOKS LIMITED
47 Church Street, Barnsley, South Yorkshire, S70 2AS, England
E-mail: enquiries@pen-and-sword.co.uk
Website: www.pen-and-sword.co.uk

Contents

Plans and Charts

CHAPTER 1

Strategic Situation May 1941 – Britain Stands Alone

Just after 11 a.m. on 18 May 1941 two massive grey shapes slipped out of the harbour of Gotenhafen (now called Gdynia) and dropped anchor in the outer roads. They were the battleship *Bismarck*, the most formidable warship in the world, and a powerful heavy cruiser, *Prinz Eugen*. They were embarking on an enterprise which was to be endowed with all the foreboding, tragedy and suspense of the most melodramatic of Wagnerian operas, leaving two of the biggest warships in the world at the bottom of the sea, with over 4,000 seamen alongside them. All this action was compressed into a period of less than ten days. It was to be a contest in which technology, luck, seamanship, airmanship and old-fashioned human grit all played a part. To understand it fully we must start by reviewing briefly the strategic situation as it existed in May 1941.

Germany had crushed the Polish forces in 1939, and Hitler's cynical pact with Stalin had allowed the division of that unfortunate country between two ruthless regimes of unparalleled savagery. Holland, Belgium and Denmark had been subdued without too much difficulty, and Norway, with its rich mineral resources, vital to the German war effort, had fallen to a brilliantly planned and executed naval and military campaign. The countries of central Europe had been recruited or dragooned onto the Axis side. Last of all, in summer 1940 France had

1

fallen to a devastating armoured and airborne assault, destroying her own army and sending the British forces in France scrambling desperately home, leaving their arms and many of their colleagues behind them. Germany was checked at the Channel, where the *Luftwaffe* was unable to establish the air superiority needed to allow German armies to force a crossing, so for the time being the land war in the West was suspended. For Germany this was not a significant check. Hitler himself was not really committed to an invasion of Britain at this point. He had other fish to fry. As the onset of autumn weather and the valour of the RAF aircrews brought a halt to the intense daytime bombing raids on southern England, his air fleets and Panzer armies redeployed in readiness for a devastating assault planned for summer 1941. This was to be against his erstwhile partner in crime – the Soviet Union.

A more active theatre of conflict for Britain now emerged in the Mediterranean. It was vital for her to retain control of the Suez Canal and of Egypt. Italian forces in Libya and Ethiopia threatened both. The Italians had at first been fairly easily defeated, but in 1941 Rommel arrived on the scene with his superb *Afrika Korps*, supported by modern aircraft. Before long, British forces were pushed back and the desperate siege of Tobruk commenced, tying down a large part of the British army, and the ships and aircraft required to supply them. The Germans also pulled Italy's chestnuts out of the fire in Greece, where local fighters had held up and indeed reversed Italian advances. The appearance of German forces in support of the Italians rapidly turned the tables. Churchill unwisely diverted the efforts of the forces facing Rommel in Egypt to support the Greek cause, and the result was a crushing defeat for Britain and the Greek patriots. In May, at the same time that *Bismarck*'s voyage was in progress, German forces had thrown the British out of mainland Greece altogether and were overrunning Crete, forcing a British withdrawal from the island, which was accomplished a few days later with heavy losses of men and material. In particular, total lack of air cover for the ships evacuating the troops resulted in disastrous losses for the British Mediterranean Fleet. Here, as everywhere, it seemed, Hitler's forces were triumphant.

It was not in Greece or in north Africa, however, that Germany presented the most deadly threat to Britain. Depending on international trade routes to supply her with arms, raw material, food and troops from her Empire, Britain was at the mercy of any enemy who could challenge her navy and close her vital sea lanes. This had very nearly happened in 1917, when U-boats had brought the country to within a few weeks of running out of food. Then only the diversion of the bulk of the destroyer force from guarding the Grand Fleet and the deployment of the little ships as escorts for convoys saved the country from being forced to sue for an ignoble peace. In 1941 it seemed that in spite of the convoy system there might be no way of averting a similar disaster.

It was not that Germany had been getting all her own way at sea. In the years leading up to the war, Germany had begun to develop a powerful surface navy, intended to be strong enough to take on that part of the Royal Navy likely to be stationed in home waters during hostilities. The naval building programme was set out in 'Plan Z'. It called for the following fleet to be built:

Type	Complete by 1948	Eventual total	Actually built or almost complete in 1939
Aircraft carrier	4	8	0
Battleship	4	4	4
Pocket battleship	9	9	3
Pocket battleship (new type)	10	12	0
Heavy cruiser	5	5	3
Light cruiser	12	24	6
Large destroyer	20	36	
Destroyer	58	70	22
Torpedo-boat	90	90	20
Submarines	241	241	57

As shown in the third column, the number of ships actually built fell far short of the plan, and left Germany with an unbalanced fleet. There were two reasons for this. Firstly Hitler had completely miscalculated the reaction of Britain and France to his invasion of Poland. He had actually promised Admiral Raeder, the chief of his navy, that there was no question of a war with Britain until 1945 at the earliest. Indeed he actually apologised to the admiral for the fact that his plans had gone wrong soon after the outbreak of the war. Secondly, as soon as war broke out the whole warship-building programme was suspended, and the labour and materials that had been allocated to surface ships were diverted to other projects. Only the U-boat programme remained intact. This left numerous half-built hulls on the stocks, notably the carrier *Graf Zeppelin* and the cruisers *Seydlitz* and *Lutzow* (which was later sold to Russia). Raeder, who had a difficult relationship with Hitler, had to make do with what ships he had. (A brief description of the organisation of the *Kriegsmarine* is given in Appendix 1.)

The demands placed on the *Kriegsmarine* were considerable, in spite of its obvious weakness. From the very first day of the war, two ancient pre-dreadnought battleships, *Schleswig-Holstein* and *Schlesien*, were pressed into service to bombard Polish shore installations. More serious for Britain were the activities of the 'pocket battleships'. These were specifically designed for commerce raiding. They had many novel design features to enable them to fulfil their role. The three ships, *Deutschland* (later renamed *Lutzow*), *Graf Spee* and *Admiral Scheer*, were all armed with six 11-inch guns. Their firepower was thus more than enough to overpower any British 8-inch cruiser fast enough to catch them, and their high speed of 28 knots enabled them to get away from a battleship should they encounter one. The only British ships that might be able to catch and out-gun them were the now aged battle cruisers, all but one of which were relics from the First World War. The ship's design was revolutionary, having all electrically welded steel hulls, and 56,800 hp diesel engines. The diesels were chosen because they were extremely economical in the cruising mode, enabling the pocket battleships to stay at sea unsupported for long periods. These ships were built in defiance of the Versailles Treaty, which limited German warships to 10,000 tons – in fact their fully loaded tonnage was over 15,000, but the Germans managed to cover this up. Reconnaissance for the pocket battleships was provided by on-board Arado float-planes.

In August 1939 two of these formidable hunters put to sea so as to be in a position to threaten the sea lanes if war should break out. On 30 September *Graf Spee* struck her first blow, sinking the British steamer *Clement*. *Deutschland* followed suit on 5 October by sinking *Stonegate*. The two raiders continued their successful *guerre de course* into October, when *Deutschland* was recalled to Germany on the direct orders of the *Führer*, who feared that she would antagonise the neutral US government, but *Graf Spee* remained on station in the Indian Ocean and the south Atlantic until November, when disaster struck her. On the 14th she intercepted and sank the small tanker *Africa Shell* off Lourenço Marques, but the tanker's crew were allowed to escape by lifeboat, and they raised the alarm as soon as they got ashore. This alerted the Royal Navy to the presence of a pocket battleship in the area, and the next victim, *Doric Star*, managed to contact patrolling British warships by radio before being sunk. Eventually, on 12 December, three cruisers, *Ajax*, *Achilles* and *Exeter*, brought the raider to battle. Although completely out-gunned by *Graf Spee*, they managed to force her to divide her fire, and damaged her structure enough to compel her to seek refuge in Montevideo harbour, Uruguay. Refused permission to repair the damage suffered at the hands of the British cruisers in the neutral port, and fearing the approach of heavy British ships, *Graf Spee*'s captain scuttled her just outside the harbour. It was the first major German loss in the war at sea and was a serious blow to the morale and prestige of the *Kriegsmarine*. *Graf Spee* had sunk some 60,000 tons of merchant shipping, but the humane and gentlemanly conduct of her captain, Langsdorff, had gained the admiration even of his victims; her loss demonstrated clearly the long reach and indomitable fighting spirit of the Royal Navy.

While these operations were in progress in the South Atlantic, Germany's heavier battleships were active further north. *Scharnhorst* and *Gneisenau* were much more formidable than the lightly armoured pocket battleships. Launched in 1936, they mounted nine 11-inch guns and displaced 38,900 tons fully loaded. They were driven by steam turbines of 165,000

horsepower, giving a top speed of 32 knots, and were protected by 14,000 tons of armour plate, 13.8 inches protecting
the armoured belt and 14.17 inches the turrets. These were
truly formidable ships, much faster than any British battleship
and better protected than any battle cruiser. They had, however,
one significant weakness. Their engines and boilers proved
extremely unreliable, resulting in long periods in dock for
repairs. In November these two powerful ships, accompanied
by a screen of light cruisers and destroyers, steamed northwards towards the Iceland–Faeroes Gap. Their object was to
attempt to divert attention from the hunt for the *Graf Spee* and
if possible to break out into the Atlantic so as to attack lightly
escorted convoys. They encountered the British armed merchant
cruiser *Rawalpindi*, which was easily disposed of in spite of a
spirited defence by her captain, Kennedy, and the crews of her
worn-out 6-inch guns. In spite of this victory, the encounter
with *Rawalpindi* was fatal to the enterprise. The German ships
were under strict instructions to avoid contact with heavy
British ships. They were aware that *Rawalpindi* had signalled
their presence to the Admiralty and that the battle cruiser
Hood, the French battleship *Dunkerque* and a number of cruisers
were searching for them, so the plan to attack Atlantic convoys
was aborted. Taking advantage of a spell of foul weather,
they slipped away and back to Wilhelmshaven. The Germans
claimed a great naval victory, but in fact this sortie only proved
how difficult it would be for significant German forces to slip
unobserved out into the north Atlantic.

The next major operation of the German fleet was the
occupation of Norway. Hitler considered this essential to the
war plans of the Reich because supplies of strategic materials
and iron ore from that region were vital to her war industries. A
reluctant Raeder was persuaded to commit almost all of his
surface fleet to transport troops and supplies to carry out the
invasion. The operation commenced on 7 April 1940. An ill-
planned Allied attempt to counter it on land was abandoned, as
the forces involved were urgently required to defend France.
The Royal Navy became aware that the German invasion fleet
was at sea almost as soon as it set out, but mistook its mission,
and deployed following a plan designed to counter another

sortie into the north Atlantic. The invasion fleet consisted of the battleships *Scharnhorst*, *Gneisenau* and *Lutzow* (previously called *Deutschland*), and the heavy cruisers *Blücher* and *Hipper*, attended by light cruisers and fourteen destroyers. Troops were successfully landed by sea and by air and achieved their objectives, but the operation was extremely costly for the *Kriegsmarine*. *Blücher* was sunk by Norwegian shore-based artillery, and her sister ship *Hipper* was rammed and heavily damaged in a suicidal attack by the destroyer *Gloworm*. *Lutzow* was hit by shore batteries and then by torpedoes from the submarine *Spearfish*. She was just able to limp home under tow, but took more than a year to repair. *Gneisenau* was hit by 15-inch shells from the battle cruiser *Renown*. Two cruisers, *Karlsruhe* and *Königsberg*, were sunk by a submarine and by air attack, and worst of all, ten of Germany's invaluable destroyers were lost in the two battles of Narvik, the second of which featured the dramatic charge into the fjord by the old battleship *Warspite*. During the course of the Allied withdrawal, the German battleships scored a major success by intercepting and sinking the carrier *Glorious*, with a full load of aircraft, off the north Norwegian coast. Some measure of revenge for this was achieved when the destroyer *Acasta* hit *Scharnhorst* with a torpedo, doing serious damage. A few days later a torpedo from the submarine *Clyde* hit *Gneisenau*, forcing her to limp home to be dry-docked. Germany emerged from the Norway operation with not one of her battleships serviceable, and almost half of her cruiser and destroyer forces were at the bottom of the sea. The resources available to Raeder at the beginning of May were reduced to the damaged heavy cruiser *Hipper*, four light cruisers and ten destroyers.

As German forces swept through France and the British Expeditionary Force was evacuated from Dunkirk, the navy had to stand idly by, suffering at the same time the annoyance of frequent bombardment in their bases by the RAF. By October the third of Hitler's pocket battleships, *Admiral Scheer*, was ready to renew the task of Atlantic raiding, and slipped out through the Denmark Strait. She was to be the most successful of all the German commerce raiders. Her first encounter was with a convoy escorted only by the armed merchant cruiser *Jervis Bay*. *Jervis Bay*'s gallant captain, Fegen, fought a hopeless action against his powerful adversary, and in doing so saved most of the merchantmen. However, *Scheer* continued her cruise, reprovisioning and refuelling from captured vessels as well as from her own support ship. She did not return to Germany until 1 April, having sunk sixteen ships totalling over 100,000 tons. It was a uniquely successful commerce-raiding cruise.

The next major sortie into the Atlantic was made by *Scharnhorst* and *Gneisenau*, repaired after their unfortunate Norwegian adventures. After a false start, during which they were damaged by bad weather, the two left Wilhelmshaven on 22 January 1941, and this time were able to slip into the Atlantic unobserved. Once again the commander of the force, Admiral Lutjens, was under strict orders not to put his ships at risk by giving battle to heavy British ships, so it was unfortunate for the commerce raiders that their first encounter was with the convoy HX 106 out of Halifax, Nova Scotia. This was escorted by the First World War battleship *Ramillies*. Though she was old and only capable of 21.5 knots, *Ramillies* had eight 15-inch guns and was very heavily armoured, so she would have been a tough opponent. The German ships drew off, and unfortunately the British lookouts misidentified *Scharnhorst* as the cruiser *Hipper*, which was also at sea further south. They failed to spot *Gneisenau* altogether. The result was a state of near-panic at the Admiralty, and *Hipper* herself was able to wreak havoc among another unescorted convoy. All available forces were sent to hunt for the raiders, and the convoy schedules were totally disrupted.

The raiders spent the next six weeks dodging British battleships and pouncing on merchantmen when they could be found. At one point they narrowly escaped an encounter with the 16-inch guns of the battleship *Rodney*, but their speed advantage of almost 10 knots enabled the Germans to escape unscathed. On another occasion they were sighted by aircraft from the carrier *Ark Royal*, but managed to make their escape. On 22 March the two ships steamed undamaged into what was to be their new home port, Brest. They had sunk twenty-one Allied ships and taken one prize. Britain had lost 115,000 tons of merchant shipping.

Raeder was delighted with the success of this cruise, and Lutjens overnight became a national hero. Ships had been sunk, convoy schedules disrupted, warships diverted from their proper tasks and confusion had reigned at the Admiralty. The whole strategy of commerce raiding with capital ships had, in Raeder's opinion, been vindicated. Better still, based in western France, his powerful ships now had easy access to the Atlantic, with no need to slip past the minefields, naval patrols and intensive air cover that plagued them when putting to sea from German or Polish bases. From Brest they could threaten not only shipping crossing the Atlantic, but also British troops and supplies *en route* for north Africa. He confidently began to make plans for another, far more ambitious mission.

Raeder, however, was seriously mistaken. In reality, in spite of the success of the cruises of the commerce raiders, by far the most serious threat to British supply lines came from submarines. At the start of the war Germany had only fifty-seven U-boats, and of these fewer than twenty were available to operate in the north Atlantic. But even this handful of boats was able to be stunningly successful, dwarfing the achievement of the surface ships. With all-volunteer crews and commanders, many of whom had served in U-boats in the First World War, the quality of the force at the disposal of Admiral Dönitz, the commander of the submarine arm, was superb. The following table gives an impression of its successes.

Dates	Number of U-boats in north Atlantic	Tonnage sunk	Losses per U-boat
June–August 1940	14	815,000	58,000
September–November 1940	12	764,000	64,000
December 1940–February 1941	10	502,000	50,200
March–May 1941	19	510,000	27,000

As well as sinking almost two million tons of merchant shipping, the U-boats had sent to the bottom the aircraft carrier *Glorious* and, by stalking into the fleet anchorage at Scapa Flow, the old battleship *Royal Oak*. U-boats had achieved far more success against the Royal Navy and had sunk almost ten times the tonnage achieved by the surface raiders for a fraction of the expenditure. In the first years of the war most of their successes had been against unescorted fast merchant ships, which the British permitted to sail independently, but by late 1940 the successful 'wolf pack' attacks on convoys had begun. These involved arranging for a pack of boats to wait for one of their number to locate a convoy, then for the whole pack to move in on it and manoeuvre into a position ahead of its track. They would then dive and wait for the convoy to pass over them. Surfacing in the middle of the convoy, preferably at night, they would each be able to account for two or three transports while the escorts tried desperately to locate the intruders. Then they would dive deep and creep away, often undetected. By May 1941, when the story of *Bismarck* begins, the U-boats had begun to suffer some reverses. British and Canadian escorts were becoming more adept at anti-submarine tactics and at using their ASDIC ('SONAR') detection systems. Aircraft were also getting better at detecting and attacking U-boats with the help of radar and improved weapons. Longer-range aircraft such as the Catalina flying-boat were coming into use. Most important of all, some of the most expert U-boat commanders were being eliminated, and their successors were seldom in the same league for cunning and expertise in their trade. The Battle of the Atlantic was still far from won, and more and more U-boats were coming into the fray, but the British could at least detect some glimmer of light at the end of the tunnel.

Access to the French Atlantic bases was a huge advantage to the U-boats, placing them nearer the Atlantic trade routes in good, deep-water harbours. It also allowed the third element in the German armoury, the long-range Condor aircraft, to operate effectively. Built as civilian airliners, and manned for the most part by their peacetime Lufthansa crews, the Condors, based in France, played no small part in the battle. They could spot for the U-boats and direct them onto targets, they could attack merchant ships themselves with a formidable load of bombs, and they could give warning of the presence of strong escorting forces.

It was not only with Germany that the Royal Navy and its allies from the Empire were contending. A fierce sea campaign was also being fought in the Mediterranean. Italy, Germany's ally, had a formidable navy. It included, at the start of the war, four old battleships and two of the magnificent Littorio class, surely the most beautiful ships of their day, each with nine 15-inch guns, and capable of 31 knots. They were superior in almost every respect to the British battleships of their day, and formed a part of a well-balanced fleet of cruisers, destroyers, naval aircraft and submarines. Fortunately for the Royal Navy, this formidable weapon was wielded with uncertain and even incompetent hands. A devastating blow was struck at it in November 1940 when two small flights of Fleet Air Arm Swordfish aircraft sank three battleships in Taranto harbour. Further damage to the fleeing survivors was then inflicted by British cruisers. (The Fleet Air Arm plays a major part in this narrative. A brief description of its development and that of RAF Coastal Command is given in Appendix 2.)

To make matters even worse for the Italians, in March 1941 a sortie by the new fast battleship *Vittorio Veneto* and a strong force of cruisers was attacked, first by torpedo-carrying Albacore and Swordfish aircraft from the carrier *Formidable*, and then at night by radar-equipped British cruisers. *Vittorio Veneto* was badly damaged by air-launched torpedoes before managing to make her escape, but no fewer than five of her supporting ships were sunk by aircraft and by gunfire from British cruisers, with the loss of 3,000 seamen. British losses were a single aeroplane. These victories enabled Britain to continue her campaign in north Africa, but the struggle was still a tough one, especially when German Ju 87 (Stuka) aircraft and U-boats joined the battle. Italy was eventually to take some revenge, also, when her midget submarines wrought havoc with British battleships in harbour in Alexandria.

CHAPTER 2

Stalemate in the West

Having briefly considered the strategic situation up to May 1941, with particular emphasis on naval affairs, we must turn our attention briefly to the political situation in so far as it is relevant to the *Bismarck*'s voyage.

France had fallen in 1940, and was divided between the German-occupied zone and Vichy France – a shameful parody of an independent regime, which slavishly followed many of the worst traits of its German overlord. French ports on the Atlantic coast were, as we have seen, open for use by German surface ships and U-boats, as were the vital ship repair yards at St Nazaire and Brest. The French navy had been a considerable force in 1939. Unlike Britain, France had embarked on an ambitious warship-building programme in the 1930s, and the two latest ships, *Richelieu* and *Jean Bart*, were far superior to the British King George V class. When France surrendered, her navy had little idea what to do. Some ships went over to General de Gaulle's Free French forces, and some surrendered themselves to the British and were interned. Others lay undecided in various north African ports. It was obviously vital to Britain that they should not fall into German hands, and every effort had to be made to prevent it. Tragically this led to the horrific action at Mers-el-Kebir, where the British fleet opened fire and destroyed a strong force of hapless French ships in harbour. No significant ships fell into German hands, but neither were they able to make a significant contribution to the British cause.

With France out of the action, Britain and her Empire were facing Germany alone, and with no significant allies. De Gaulle's Free French movement was supported by some of France's colonies in central Africa, but its relationship with the British government was difficult, and in any case it had very little of importance to contribute to the cause. French colonies in north Africa and the Levant sided with Vichy, and fought against British forces in the area.

In central Europe, Austria, Hungary, Romania and Bulgaria were all in full co-operation with the Axis powers. Czechoslovakia's substantial heavy industries were at Hitler's disposal. In Spain General Franco had been enabled to achieve power as a result of Hitler's assistance, and the *Führer* expected his help in return to complete the alliance against Britain. However, the *Generalissimo* was no fool, and he showed himself to be a tough negotiator. The last thing he wanted was a German army loose in his country, or U-boats based in his ports antagonising the US government. He set an impossibly high price on any assistance he might give to Germany, and Hitler walked away from his talks with Franco, saying that he would have preferred a visit to the dentist. Franco's obduracy was critical to the British cause. Had he co-operated, as Hitler had hoped, Gibraltar would have fallen, denying Britain access to the Mediterranean, and U-boats in Spanish ports could have operated without fear of the attentions of the RAF.

Of Britain's Dominions, by far the most important in the war at sea was Canada. The Royal Canadian Navy had been an insignificant force until 1939, and at the outbreak of the war it consisted of thirteen small ships and 3,000 men. There was no centralised command structure between it and the Royal Navy, and the Canadians had no assigned role to fulfil in the event of war. When it came, however, the Dominion responded magnificently. By the end of the war the RCN had increased to 373 ships and 90,000 men. This rapid expansion naturally led to some very inexperienced crews putting to sea in the early stages of the conflict. However, Canada played a vital role in guarding convoys on the western side of the Atlantic. Canada too made an enormous contribution to the Allied ship-building effort. In an incredibly short space of time the Canadians organised themselves to build merchant ships to replace some of those lost in combat, and also escorts such as the Flower Class corvettes that played a key part in defeating the U-boats.

Apart from the Empire, however, there were no allies, and Britain stood alone against the Fascist monster which now dominated Europe.

There were, of course, in the first half of 1941 two 'Elephants in the room' – uncommitted major powers. The Soviet Union was bound to Germany by the Hitler–Stalin pact, and in spite of many intelligence indications to the contrary, Stalin resolutely refused to believe that Hitler was about to break it. The annexation of Poland and the Baltic States had been successful for both parties, and the Soviets now seemed more interested in stamping out any spark of opposition to their own brutal rule than to safeguarding their country from any forthcoming German assault. Even a cursory reading of Hitler's published works would have shown them how mistaken this policy was. In fact, during 1940 and the first part of 1941, the USSR was inclined to be hostile to the British cause, and in any case had nothing to contribute to the naval campaign.

That left the USA, already by far the largest and most advanced industrial power in the world. By mid-1941 the country was slowly coming round to the belief that the British cause was not hopeless (in spite of the reports of the odious Ambassador Kennedy), and that it deserved her support. The US constitution specifically warns the nation against 'entangling alliances', and in 1939 most Americans probably wanted to stay out of the war. Many prominent citizens – Lindbergh, the legendary aviator, for example – actually favoured the Nazi cause. President Roosevelt himself instinctively hated everything he knew about Hitler's regime and wanted to help to put a stop to its military triumphs. He had also developed a warm personal relationship with Churchill, but he was a canny politician and knew better than to get ahead of public opinion or to try to lead the Congress in a direction in which it was not ready to go. Also, he had won an election in November 1940 partly on the basis of keeping his country out of the war. Fortunately, by 1941 voices more favourable to Britain were working on the US electorate. The most important of these was Ed Morrow, whose regular news bulletins from London during the Battle of Britain and the Blitz were hugely influential, giving the impression of a nation united and determined to stand against the European dictators.

As early as 1939, a neutrality act was introduced, which called for US ships to patrol a neutrality zone extending 300 miles from the coast. In November of that year the embargo on trade in arms with the belligerent states was lifted, and this greatly favoured Britain and France, as it was impossible for Germany to obtain shipments of arms from across the Atlantic. Massive orders for vehicles and armaments were placed, incidentally helping to lift US industry out of recession. When France fell, Britain took over the orders placed by the French. As promised by the President soon after his re-election, America was becoming the 'arsenal of democracy', and it suited the President's policy and his people's pockets. In June 1940 Roosevelt went further and launched a billion-dollar rearmament campaign aimed mainly at the threat of Japanese expansion in the Pacific. This was followed by a further programme specific to the US Navy. Britain worked hard to convince the President that with the help of surplus, even obsolescent, American equipment, it could guard the Atlantic 'back door' of the USA while the new warships to be built could concentrate in the Pacific. This led in September 1940 to the release of fifty First World War four-stack destroyers to Britain to help with convoy escort duties, in return for the use of eight British possessions by American forces. (In fact the destroyers were in such poor shape that it was many months before they came into service.) Staff talks at a senior level between the US Navy and the Royal Navy began. In March 1941 the Lend-Lease Act gave the President authority to supply whatever military equipment was needed to any power whose cause he considered important to US security without seeking immediate payment for it. One of the prime considerations from the US point of view was to prevent any danger of the British fleet falling into German hands if Britain had to make a dishonourable peace with the Nazis. Gradually the USA was being drawn into the war on the British side. More and more public opinion in America was being alienated from Germany by the sinking of merchant ships by U-boats.

American naval vessels were becoming more aggressive in asserting their 300-mile limit, which was extended in April to cover a much larger area of the Atlantic. German naval commanders were certain that the USA was co-operating closely with the Royal Navy and doing everything short of open war to help the British cause. In reality this was an exaggerated opinion. Roosevelt was careful not to go beyond the bounds of neutrality. In the end he did not have to declare war on Germany, as Hitler declared war on him after Pearl Harbor. Nevertheless, by the time of *Bismarck*'s voyage, the might of US industry, in particular US-built aircraft, was playing a key role in the struggle. The US Navy even went as far as to carry out a little clandestine spotting of U-boats for the British.

The picture in May 1941 is of Britain stretched to the limit, without allies and with little hope of victory, down but not quite out. She could survive provided that merchant shipping losses could be contained and material support from the USA and the Empire continued. Without it she was doomed.

How had Britain been reduced to such a weak military condition? The period between 1919 and 1939 has been described as 'the long weekend'. It was a period in which the country basked in a complacent spell of wishful thinking and unrealistic optimism. Defence affairs were conducted on the assumption that any international dispute could be solved by the League of Nations, and armed conflict was unthinkable. The 'ten-year rule' demanded that defence policy should be conducted on the assumption that there would be no war for at least ten years, and was automatically renewed annually. Aircraft, ships and tanks were developed in a lackadaisical, penny-pinching way, and numbers built were pitifully small. Worst of all, as regards the Royal Navy, Britain stuck rigidly to treaty limitations on the number, size and armament of ships, so that the few that were built were to be totally out-classed by those of Germany, Italy and Japan, who disregarded or circumvented internationally agreed treaties. These were the Washington Naval Treaty of 1922 and the Geneva and London Agreements of the 1930s, in which the British and American governments pledged themselves to 'take risks for peace'. (A brief description of the treaties is given in Appendix 4.) Even when Hitler was known to be developing submarines, warships and, with the co-operation of the Soviet Union, aircraft and tanks that were to form the basis of the formidable army destined to dominate Europe, it was easier for British politicians to turn a blind eye. 'Hitler is a reasonable man' was the theory. 'Anyway, better him than Bolshevism – after all the Germans are essentially decent people with whom we can work.' This rubbish was peddled by Liberals and Conservatives, and Labour, though less hostile to Communism, was especially wedded to pacifist principles. There were a few, notably Churchill, who argued otherwise, but he was far from the centre of power. The following chapters will illustrate some of the results of this 'long weekend' as far as the *Bismarck* episode is concerned.

Chapter 3

Operation Rhine Exercise

The relative success of the cruise of *Scharnhorst* and *Gneisenau* had left Raeder elated, and it did not take him long to formulate a plan to exploit its achievements. If two relatively lightly armed battleships could do such damage and cause such chaos to Atlantic shipping, what could a strong battle squadron supported by supply ships and tankers do? Suppose the raiders did not need to run away from a battleship escort, but could fight it out and at the same time destroy the convoy? What countermeasures could the British then take? If they did manage to get together enough heavy ships and aircraft carriers to threaten his ships, his raiders could use their speed to make a dash for the safety of their French ports and shore-based air cover. For a number of reasons it was urgent to seize the moment. Firstly, as we have seen, the Germans firmly believed that the USA was moving gradually towards joining the British war effort. If this happened the raiding group would be facing attack from both sides of the Atlantic and the chances of success would be much diminished. Secondly, there were political imperatives within Germany. Raeder was never close to Hitler, and was facing constant criticism from him. He was far too much the old-style German officer for Hitler's taste, and the *Führer*, understanding nothing of the sea, had no sympathy with the problems that his Grand Admiral faced. There seemed, in Hitler's eyes, to be a stark contrast between his armies, victorious everywhere, and his navy, which had already lost two major units (*Blucher* and *Graf Spee*), and most of the others were so damaged that they were out of action for many months. Raeder was aware of the forthcoming assault on Russia, and was determined to gain a major victory at sea so as not to fall yet further behind the army in prestige. There had already been dark hints that the navy was consuming labour and raw materials that could be better used elsewhere. Why not give up the surface fleet altogether and use the men and precious raw materials where they would do most good? At the same time as criticising his navy, Hitler continually urged caution on its commander. His warships were to avoid encounters with equal or superior British forces. He could not afford to lose another ship. 'I am a hero on land,' he boasted, 'at sea I am a coward.'

Even within the navy itself there were doubts about the surface fleet. Dönitz, the redoubtable commander of the U-boat force, in theory reported to Raeder but in practice did almost as he wanted. He too had doubts about the heavy ships. The effort and materials going into a single battleship could have built more than fifty U-boats, and the damage done to Allied shipping would have been far greater. Dönitz was much more Hitler's type of man than Raeder. The *Führer* always treated his U-boat commander with respect and avoided the sort of screaming confrontation with him that characterised his relationship with other leaders. It almost seemed that Hitler was a little in awe of Dönitz.

All these factors piled pressure on Raeder as he planned what was to become known as Operation Rhine Exercise (*Rheinübung*). The plan was ambitious. *Bismarck* and *Tirpitz* – two new super-battleships – far superior to any warship that the British could muster to fight them, supported by cruisers, would sneak out from the Baltic, and join up with *Scharnhorst* and *Gneisenau*, which could put to sea from their French ports. The enemy could not quickly put together a force able to counter this, and so the German ships could cruise the Atlantic at leisure, cutting off once and for all Britain's lines of communication. They would be sustained at sea by a small fleet of supply ships and oilers lurking in the Atlantic, and of course, if they were lucky, they might be able to seize supplies from captured ships. If by any mischance they came across a strong British battle squadron, all the German ships had speeds in excess of 30 knots and could show a clean pair of heels to any British battleship. The plan was superficially attractive, but Hitler didn't like it. What about attack from aircraft carriers? What about British submarines? Raeder, not easily deterred, batted away the objections and continued with his plans. He was rapidly finding that it was as important to stop details of his plan from leaking out within German government circles, where there were plenty of people wanting to sabotage it, as it was to keep it from the enemy. Unfortunately for him, arrangements for Rhine Exercise began to go awry almost as soon as they were made.

Raeder's scheme was very time dependent. Rhine Exercise had to take place before the Russian campaign was launched, and before America joined the war. It also had to be in the summer months, otherwise weather in the northern waters would be too violent and the nights too long to allow much action. As spring 1941 drew on, the urgency increased, but at the same time more and more things began to go wrong. The first problem was *Tirpitz*. Although she had been launched in April 1939 and completed in February 1941, she was clearly not going to be ready for a combat mission in May. Plagued by mechanical and 'systems' problems, she was still working-up in the Baltic, and had to be left out of the picture. The next was *Scharnhorst*. Her problem was with her Wagner extra-high-pressure boilers. They were a constant source of trouble and had to be practically rebuilt in Brest, but this was a long process and she could not be ready for sea for several months. In fact, Free French agents in Brest had seen the boiler tubes being removed and reported this to London, so it was no secret to the British. The repair process was not helped by the RAF's bombing raids on the port, which were frequent and heavy. The final casualty was *Gneisenau*. She had a different type of boiler and was fit for sea, but on 4 April an RAF bomb fell between her and the dockside without exploding. Bomb-disposal experts decided that it would be too dangerous to defuse the bomb with *Gneisenau* in dock, and she was moved out onto a buoy in the harbour. She was near the north shore with high ground to the north of her, and a mole that ran out from the seaward side gave her protection and shelter. On her mooring she was heavily protected by flak ships and by shore-based anti-aircraft guns. In spite of this, as soon as her move was reported to the Admiralty by French resistance workers, and her position had been confirmed by photographs taken by a high-flying reconnaissance Spitfire, it became plain that the move had made her more vulnerable. On 6 April a flight of three Coastal Command Beaufort torpedo-bombers set out to attack her. The Beaufort was not the most inspired of aircraft designs, but it had the range to reach Brest from England and was a reasonably steady torpedo platform. The flight got split up in poor visibility, and the concentrated attack planned for the three aircraft attacking together did not materialise. One aircraft, however, arriving after the others, and piloted by Flying Officer Kenneth Campbell, came in only fifty feet above the water and appeared over the mole when the gunners believed that the attack was over. The aircraft had to slow down to 90 knots and drop its torpedo from a position close to the mole, less than 500 yards from the target. The Beaufort would then normally have applied full power and jinked away at low level to avoid anti-aircraft fire. In this instance the high ground behind the target forced Campbell to bank sharply and climb as soon as he had launched his weapon. This presented an easy target, and the plane was shot down into the harbour, killing all the occupants. The torpedo, however, ran true and blew the stern of the unfortunate *Gneisenau* to pieces. French resistance reported Campbell's gallantry to London and he was awarded a posthumous VC. *Gneisenau* was moved back into dock, where she suffered the indignity of being hit again, this time by high-level bombs. She was out of action for six critical months.

Raeder was thus left with only *Bismarck* and one brand-new heavy cruiser, *Prinz Eugen*, to carry out his cherished Rhine Exercise. It is important now to consider what a risky mission was in prospect. British, American, Japanese or Italian capital ships would never operate without an entourage of destroyers or light cruisers to cover them from attack by aircraft, submarines and enemy light forces. In most cases, if they were to be out of reach of land-based aircraft, they would have a carrier escort as well. But here was Raeder, having lost most of his destroyers and light cruisers, proposing to send the largest and probably the most costly warship ever built into a hostile north Atlantic with no air cover whatever and, once she was outside friendly waters, no destroyer escort. It is difficult to avoid the term 'foolhardy'. The designated force commander, Lutjens, more or less told him this. But Raeder was a stubborn character, determined to redeem the reputation of the service that he commanded. Operation Rhine Exercise would go ahead. The operational order for Rhine Exercise, dated 2 April 1941, envisaged *Gneisenau* emerging to create a diversion by operating alone in the south Atlantic, but this order, of course, was issued before the successful torpedo attack. It also acknowledged that difficulties would be presented due to *Prinz Eugen*'s limited range, but stated that this would be overcome by refuelling at sea. It also referred to the potential of her formidable torpedo armament. She had no fewer than twelve torpedo tubes that could be used against enemy capital ships detected at close range. Co-operation with U-boats was called for in the order, suggesting that they should be used to scout for the surface ships, and appropriate arrangements for communication between U-boats and the two surface ships were made. Significantly there was not a single mention in the order of air support.

At this point we must pause in the story of *Bismarck*'s voyage and consider the ships, aircraft and men who were to participate in the conflict.

First *Bismarck* herself. The following statistics compare her to the three heavy British ships she would encounter. (A fuller description of *Bismarck* is given in Appendix 3.)

	Bismarck	*Hood*	*King George V* and *Prince of Wales*	*Rodney*
Length	813 ft	860 ft	745 ft	710 ft
Beam	118 ft	104 ft	103 ft	106 ft
Displacement	50,900 tons	45,200 tons	40,580 tons	38,000 tons
Armament	8×15 in.	8×15 in.	10×14 in.	9×16 in.
Armour wt	17,000 tons	13,800 tons	12,000 tons	n/a
Belt	12.6 in.	12 in.	15 in.	14 in.
Turrets	14.7 in.	15 in.	16 in.	16 in.
Deck	4.72 in.	3 in.	6 in.	6.25 in.
Speed	30.8 kts	32 kts	28 kts	23.8 kts
Launch date	1940	1918	1939	1925
Engine Power	138,000 shp	151,000 shp	110,000 shp	45,000 shp

Perhaps the most significant line in the table is the launch date. *Bismarck* was in almost every respect a more advanced ship that any of her opponents. It is an interesting fact that two-thirds of the thirty-five capital ships sunk in the Second World War pre-dated the Washington Treaty. Putting this another way, obsolescent vessels were almost invariably the most vulnerable. *Bismarck's* main armament could fire a little over two rounds per minute at a velocity of 890 yards per second, and achieve a range of 38,700 yards – almost twenty-two miles – out-ranging *Hood* by 8,000 yards. Following the tradition of earlier German battleships, she had a very broad beam, making her a stable gun platform and allowing space for good underwater anti-torpedo armour. To direct the fire of her massive armament, like all other battleships of the time, she had centralised fire-control systems. Hers used either the 11.5-yard optical range-finders, of which there were five, two mounted in rotating cupolas and three within the gun turrets, or, in bad visibility, she could use the Seetakt radar directors. Information from the range and direction finders was fed into the fire-control station mounted high above the bridge, where the gunnery officer and his staff used an electromechanical computer system to handle the mass of data needed to direct the guns. Accurate fire at long range from a ship that might be moving at 30 knots at a target whose course and speed were difficult to observe accurately was an extremely tricky operation. Admiral Cunningham, probably the most able Allied naval commander of the war, once remarked that he couldn't understand how naval guns ever managed to hit anything at all. A shell might take thirty seconds or so to reach its target, during which time the target itself might cover 400 yards. The flight of the missile would also be effected by wind speed and direction, the roll of the ship, humidity and a host of other factors. This meant that the process of aiming and firing the guns was extremely complex, and required highly trained and practised gunnery teams. The Germans had superbly trained gunnery staff, and regularly found the range and hit their targets more rapidly than their opponents. This was partly due to the long and arduous work-up routines in the Baltic, which the German navy in both world wars insisted on, and partly to the excellent quality of the optical instruments used.

As close-range protection against surface attack, *Bismarck* had twelve 5.9-inch quick firers, and for long-range anti-aircraft use, sixteen 4.1-inch high-angle weapons and twenty-eight smaller-calibre close-range guns. Also, for anti-aircraft purposes she could depress her main armament so that it fired into the sea close to the ship's side, throwing up huge walls of water that would wreck any incoming plane that hit it.

Her main engines were three Blohm and Voss geared turbines turning three shafts and developing 138,000 shaft horsepower. Eight thousand tons of oil fuel was carried, giving a cruising range of 9,280 nautical miles. For reconnaissance she could carry four seaplanes, which were launched from catapults and recovered from the water by crane. The hull was divided into twenty-one watertight compartments, so that she was extremely resilient to damage from gunfire, mines or torpedoes.

Unlike the British warships built between the wars, she was a 'no compromise' battleship, the very best Germany could build, taking no account of treaty limitations and very little of cost. Like the German battle cruisers and battleships of the First World War, she was to prove incredibly tough and difficult to sink. However, she had some significant weaknesses.

Bismarck had three radars, all essentially similar. These were known as the FuMO or Seetakt systems. This radar system was essentially a gun-ranging device only. The Seetakt had very limited capacity for sea search or anti-aircraft duties. In most conditions its range was only about twelve miles. The gunnery team found that except in very thick weather or total darkness gun direction by radar was less accurate than by visual systems. Only in the worst conditions was the Seetakt superior to visual rangefinders. The system was also so delicate that if the main armament was fired, the vibrations almost always put the radar out of operation. Another system worked alongside it to monitor hostile radar transmissions. This was effective, but, as we shall see, could sometimes be misleading. The reason for this crucial lack of attention to a vital area of development lies deep in the heart of inter-service and industrial rivalry in 1930s Germany. The German navy had demonstrated a working radar gun-ranging system in the 1920s, long before Britain had evolved such a device, but development of radar was divided between the navy and the *Luftwaffe*, each of which jealously guarded its secrets from the other. They contracted out radar development to different industrial organisations. The result was that Germany entered the war with extremely poor marine radar systems, and although the *Luftwaffe* had developed an excellent mobile radar, it was not used at sea and was not deployed to maximum advantage on land either. Furthermore, German intelligence was not aware of the strides that Britain was making in radar development, and this laid their armed forces open to some nasty surprises at sea and in the air.

Another weakness was within the ship herself. *Bismarck's* design was heavily influenced by that of the Bayen Class battleships, which were completed in 1916. In order to keep the draft of these ships shallow enough to allow them to pass through the Kiel Canal, they had twin balanced rudders positioned well above the level of the keel, in place of the single central rudder normally used on other nations' battleships. On trials it was noticed that this made the ship impossible to steer using the engines alone, and her captain noted that the steering-gear was vulnerable to torpedo attack. The rudders were power operated, with an emergency system allowing them to be manually operated from the stern of the ship if the power steering was damaged, but this manual operation was not really practical. It involved the whole crew of the aft gun turret abandoning their posts to work the rudders, and organising this proved extremely difficult even during practice drills in calm water. In action it would be dangerous and impractical.

Experts have argued that *Bismarck's* armour was not well distributed. The King George V Class British battleships had very heavy armour over critical areas such as magazines and engines, and less over non vital areas of the hull. *Bismarck's* armour was more widely distributed over the hull and gave less concentrated protection to vital areas. This may be a justified criticism, but in practice no weakness in her armour seems to have been apparent. She was subject to some fearsome punishment during her voyage, and the critical damage she suffered was certainly not attributable to lack of protection of engines, magazines or main armament.

Finally the anti-aircraft armament was not satisfactory. The 5.9-inch guns could only achieve about six rounds per minute, which was too slow for effective anti-aircraft fire, and the 4.1s had a fatal flaw in their fire-director system. This aimed them at the target as seen from the director, taking no account of the fact that the actual gun might be over 100 yards away from the director itself. In addition, the whole flak-direction centre was poorly designed and vulnerable to damage from shock. It has been suggested that the combination of 5.9-inch and 4.1-inch guns was wasteful and that all-purpose secondary armament would have been more effective. Certainly results showed that her anti-aircraft systems were not as efficient as they might have been, but that can be said of all battleships built before the devastating effectiveness of air power was demonstrated in the Second World War. These weaknesses were to play a part in the tragic voyage of the great ship.

During her working-up period in the Baltic, *Bismarck* normally pretended she was engaged with the British battle cruiser *Hood*. This was because *Hood* was in many respects regarded as the pride of the Royal Navy, and she was indeed one of the very few British capital ships that would be able to catch up with her and bring her to battle. In reality there was little comparison between the two. *Hood* was very much in the tradition of the First World War British battle cruisers – fast, heavily armed, but extremely vulnerable and quite unfit to compete with a battle-ship. She was, however, the 'crack ship' of the Royal Navy, being large, fast and impressive to see, and she had 'carried the flag' to ports and naval reviews all over the world. It was always considered a great privilege to serve on her. Although she was laid down in September 1916 – four months after the Battle of Jutland – it was clear that the lessons of that conflict had not been properly learnt. Her deck armour was insufficient to keep out plunging shells, and vital systems were poorly protected. There were programmes to correct some of these faults, but not all of them were implemented, partly to save cost and partly because the ship was so heavily engaged on 'showing-the-flag' missions that she had little time in dock to allow modifications to be made. Another critical fault was her gunnery-direction system. This was based on the design adopted, in the face of expert advice, before the First World War. *Hood* was in fact the only ship in the Royal Navy fitted with what was called the Mark V Dreyer table, an electromechanical analogue computer designed to make the calculations required to aim the guns. The system was extremely complicated and naturally depended for its accuracy both on skilful operators and on accurate inputs. The inputs were often the problem. The 30-foot rangefinders were inferior to the German 34-foot system both because of their shorter base-line and because of their inferior optics. The German system calculated the range by showing two images of the target, which the observer would superimpose, one on the other, to find the range. The British system required the observer to find a vertical feature such as a mast or funnel on the enemy ship and adjust the rangefinder until it appeared unbroken. In practice this was very much more difficult to operate. The other drawback of the Dreyer system was that it was relatively slow to operate, so that changes in speed or bearing of the enemy were often adjusted for far too late to allow the aim to be corrected. Unlike *Bismarck*, *Hood* does not appear to have had independent fire-control computing systems in the turrets for emergency use.

Hood was, in summary, a First World War ship trying to fight in the Second World War. Any contact with a modern battleship could only have one result.

We now turn to the British battleships arrayed against the *Kriegsmarine*'s powerful new fleet. At the outbreak of the Second World War, Britain had twelve battleships in service. Of these no fewer than ten had served in the First World War, and although they had been quite extensively modernised and in most cases fitted with radar, they were woefully obsolete by 1939. The five Queen Elizabeth Class 'fast battleships' had been laid down in 1912 and 1913, and completed in 1914 and 1915. Four of them had actually fought at Jutland, in May 1916. They had eight 15-inch guns and a top speed of 24 knots. The five Royal Sovereign Class ships of the 1913 programme were completed in 1916 and 1917 and were designed to be part of the main battle fleet. They had the same main armament but were even slower than the Queen Elizabeths, only achieving 21 knots. This was adequate in 1916 but hopeless in 1939, when enemy battleships were almost ten knots faster. How had Britain come to depend on such ancient and inadequate vessels for her defence? The reason is not far to seek. Britain had spent the inter-war years basking in her blissful fog of wishful thinking as far as defence was concerned, planning, as we have seen, on the basis of no possibility of war for ten years. Any naval ship-building had to conform rigidly to treaty obligations. (A fuller account of the naval treaties is given in Appendix 4.) Further-more, budgetary constraints meant that the numbing influence of the Treasury intruded into naval affairs, with its usual debilitating results. The outcome was two generations of rather unsatisfactory battleships.

The King George V Class, which included the *Prince of Wales*, consisted of five ships, all laid down in 1937, the first ship, *King George V* herself, becoming operational in January 1941. They were built and commissioned in a great rush, and mounted 14-inch main armament, as this enabled them to be constructed quickly and cheaply. They were found to be sadly lacking in anti-aircraft capability, although they were better armed in this respect than *Bismarck*. They did have some improvements over previous warships in that vital parts of the ships were well protected with up to fifteen inches of armour, and they had the AFCT-type gunnery-control system, which was faster and more efficient than the Dreyer equipment. They had various different radar fits, *Prince of Wales*, for example, having the Type 281 set, which was mainly intended for air-attack warning, but also had limited surface-ship search capability. It could also be used for gun ranging. The main shortcoming of these ships, apart from the lack of AA capability, which was not relevant to the *Bismarck* operation, was their relatively slow speed. 110,000 shp was not enough to enable them to keep up with the German or Italian battleships against which they would have to fight. Their maxi-mum speed of 28 knots was some three knots too slow.

The other battleships built between the wars were the Nelson Class, consisting of two ships, *Nelson* and *Rodney*, both launched in 1925. These were truly astonishing-looking vessels, with all nine 16-inch guns mounted in three turrets forward of the bridge. To conform to treaty requirements, their machinery weight was cut to a minimum, so that they were absurdly slow (23.8 knots when new), and had very erratic handling, requiring up to twelve degrees of rudder even to keep straight in a moderate headwind. Their peculiar layout brought grave operational disadvantages. The guns could not be fired when traversed to point anywhere aft of the beam, as the blast would destroy their own bridge structure, nor could they be fired straight ahead, because the shock-wave caused by the recoil would damage the structure of the ship. However, they were very heavily armed and well protected. The weight of their broadside was thirty per cent greater than *Bismarck*'s, and if these ships could only catch up with their foe they stood a good chance of outfighting her. In fact this chimed in well with current British naval thinking concerning the use of air power. Naval aircraft would wing the enemy so as to slow him down, and then the battleships would catch up and finish him off. The slow speed of the British battleships at Matapan invalidated this theory, however, as the Italian battleship *Vittorio Veneto*, though 'winged', was able to outrun the three Queen Elizabeths trying to catch her. We shall see how it applied to the fight with the *Bismarck*.

Cruisers played important roles in the conflict, and we should briefly examine the ships primarily involved:

	Prinz Eugen	*Suffolk*	*Norfolk*	*Sheffield*
Length	675 ft	630 ft	610 ft	558 ft
Beam	70 ft	68 ft	66 ft	62 ft
Displacement	14,050 tons	9,750 tons	10,035 tons	9,100 tons
Armament	8 × 8 in.	8 × 8 in.	8 × 8 in.	12 × 6 in.
Speed	32 kts	31.5 kts	31.5 kts	32 kts
Launch date	1940	1926	1928	1936

Other heavy British cruisers similar to *Norfolk* were involved in the final stages of the conflict. It is fairly obvious that *Prinz Eugen* was a larger and better protected ship than any of the British cruisers. Almost all her extra weight was devoted to protective armour and to secondary armament. Like *Bismarck*, she had extremely efficient optical rangefinding and fire-direction gear, and her gunnery seems to have been excellent.

There was one crucial area in which the British ships were superior – radar. *Prinz Eugen* had the same Seetakt radar as *Bismarck*, although actually it seems to have been more reliable, possibly because it had to endure less shock from the recoil of the ship's guns. *Sheffield* had Type 79Y radar, which had very limited search range and was one of the earliest British ship-mounted radars. Her radar team, however, seems to have been very skilful, and her set was used for aircraft early warning and fighter direction when she was working in conjunction with aircraft carriers, which in the early stages of the war had no radar at all. *Norfolk* had a more modern Type 286M millimetric target-indication radar, which was primarily designed for aircraft early warning. For this role it was very advanced for its day, but its surface-ship search range was limited. *Suffolk*'s Type 284 radar was newly fitted and was specifically designed for gun control and surface-ship search, with a range of up to twenty miles. It had a system known as lobe switching, which enabled it to give very accurate bearings to the target. Far more advanced than any set the Germans had encountered or imagined at the time, this was to play a key part in the battle. The Royal Navy had showed itself surprisingly nimble in adopting radar (confusingly then called RDF) to its needs for gun direction and aiming, as well as for anti-aircraft duties. As early as February 1940 the battleship *Nelson* was able to report that she could range her guns accurately at 30,000 yards using her new 'RDF' set, and the pace of development, involving naval and RAF officers working in harness with civilian scientists, was extraordinarily impressive. The 'press gangs' who had made the navy notorious in previous centuries would have admired the success that their successors in the 1930s achieved in getting the best brains from the universities (mostly from Cambridge) to work on the most complex of scientific problems related to electronic warfare..

Aircraft played a critical part in the *Bismarck* encounter, at least on the British side. Many RAF and naval types were used for various purposes during the hunt, the most important being listed below. German air involvement was surprisingly absent and ineffective. Fw 200 Condors, based on the Biscay coast, had a range of 2,700 miles and could easily have reached the scene of the latter stages of the conflict. However, they would have been able to do very little when they got there, as they were essentially civilian airliners and therefore too vulnerable to risk attacking warships. No *Luftwaffe* land-based aircraft became involved until the final stages of the conflict. Much of the time they were grounded by bad weather – although, as we shall see, this 'bad weather' did not prevent the Fleet Air Arm from flying off aircraft carriers.

Principle types of aircraft employed were:

	Arado 196	Catalina	Swordfish
Role	Recon-fighter	Recon-bomber	Torpedo-bomber
Range	665 miles	2,545 miles	546 miles
Speed	200 mph	190 mph	138 mph
Crew	2	Typically 9	2 or 3

The Arado was a fast float-plane intended for reconnaissance, but it was also heavily armed with forward-facing cannon and rear-facing machine-guns, and it could carry a useful bomb load. *Bismarck* carried four Arados and *Prinz Eugen* three. They were launched by catapult and recovered by means of a crane. In trials the crane on *Bismarck* had proved rather unreliable. In several instances Arados gave an excellent account of themselves in battle, being very agile for a float-plane.

The Catalina was one of the most important Allied aircraft of the war, playing a vital anti-shipping and anti-submarine role in the Atlantic and the Pacific. It had an extremely long endurance – almost twenty-four hours when an auxiliary fuel tank was used. The high wing configuration gave the crew excellent downward visibility. Armament varied but was normally five machine-guns and 4,000 lb of bombs or depth charges.

The Swordfish looked like an aircraft from the First World War, with its large biplane design and open cockpits. In fact it was a fairly recent design – the first had flown only in 1934, and it proved to be a highly effective torpedo-bomber – rugged, stable and easy to fly on and off an aircraft carrier. The crew of three consisted of pilot, observer, and gunner/signaller, although in some cases the gun, which was practically useless, was dispensed with. Although it was painfully slow (the 130 mph maximum speed was hardly ever achieved in practice – 90 mph was more realistic when the plane was fully loaded), the Swordfish was so manoeuvrable that it could often shake off pursuing fighters by going down to a few feet above the sea. It would then make a series of rapid turns which high-performance aircraft could not follow. Of course this tactic would not have worked against experienced pilots in agile aircraft. One technique used by German pilots was to lower their flaps and undercarriages when making an attack so as to reduce stalling speed, enabling successful attacks to be made on slow-flying aircraft. However, the slow-speed weaving tactic was effectively used many times in the Mediterranean. At least once a Swordfish caused two Italian fighters to crash into the sea by using this tactic. When flying through flak, often the Swordfish's very slow speed and agility would confuse gunners, and its fabric-covered wings and fuselage could absorb many hits without fatal damage. Explosive ordnance would often pass through the fabric surfaces without detonating. Although the structure of the 'Stringbag' looked frail, the machines were actually surprisingly tough, using steel bracing-wires and structural components. Swordfish were used as dive-bombers, minelayers, reconnaissance aircraft and to depth charge submarines, but their most effective role was as torpedo carriers. Their superb low-level handling meant that they could come in only feet above the sea, at which level the target ship's guns often would not bear. Even if the guns did bear, an attacker so close to the sea surface was difficult to see and aim at, as there was no silhouette against the sky. British 18-inch air-dropped torpedoes had to be delivered at 90 mph or less and from very low levels, flying straight at the target, and so a slow aircraft, close to the surface, manned by a crew with steady nerves, was the ideal torpedo-bomber. Having dropped his torpedo, the Swordfish pilot could turn sharply away from the target without losing height or banking (banking needed to be avoided if possible, as it would have the effect of presenting an easier target to enemy gunners). When dive-bombing, the Swordfish could carry up to 2,000 lb of bombs. It could dive very steeply at about 200 knots without getting out of control, then pull out only a few feet above the target. By 1941 some Swordfish were fitted with an ASV (air-to-surface-vessel) radar set mounted between the wheels of the fixed undercarriage. This was primarily for anti-submarine work but was also useful for locating surface-ships, or indeed the home carrier herself in thick weather. The carrier *Ark Royal's* Swordfish crews were very experienced, having fought in the Mediterranean and the Atlantic for a long period. As we shall see, they played a decisive role in the battle.

We should now turn to some of the key senior involved in the conflict. Admiral Raeder does not come across as an attractive personality. Born in 1876, he was 64 at the time of the *Bismarck* engagement, and every inch a traditional Imperial German naval officer. He was extremely strict and formal with his subordinates, a stickler for detail and intolerant of criticism in any form. This soon led him into conflict with Hitler, who disliked him, and with Göring, who successfully resisted the navy's demands for a dedicated naval air service and ensured that the *Luftwaffe* rendered the navy minimal operational support, except when he himself could claim all the credit. Raeder had served with distinction on the gallant battle cruiser *Seydlitz* through most her actions during the First World War, and was one of the small group of mid-ranking naval officers selected to remain in the service throughout the inter-war period, becoming head of the navy in 1928. He was promoted Grand Admiral in 1939 – the first to hold this post since the great Tirpitz. As supreme head of the navy he was famous for his hard work, his close personal supervision of all operations and for his excessive secrecy. His subordinates were allowed little scope to use their own initiative. He communicated with Hitler as little as he could and enraged the *Führer* by seldom telling him about any operation until it had actually been launched and could not be changed. He does not seem to have been a committed Nazi, but he supported the Hitler regime because it promised to rebuild the navy to which he had devoted his life.

Responsibility for Operation Rhine Exercise and its ultimate failure rests squarely on his shoulders.

Raeder selected an admiral cast in some respects in his own mould to lead the operation. Lutjens was a highly decorated commander of torpedo boats in the First World War, receiving among other decorations the Knight's Cross of the Royal House of Hohenzollern. Remaining in the navy after the war, he first specialised in torpedo boat operations, then took up various staff jobs. In 1940 he found himself admiral commanding scouting forces, and was actively involved in the successful Norway operation. He was anything but a charismatic character, insisting on making decisions himself without consulting his staff, and seldom talking to anyone except when he had to. Like Raeder, he disliked the Nazi ideal and he risked his career by bravely protesting against the persecution of Jewish citizens. Famously he refused to use the Nazi salute, preferring the traditional navy hand to the cap. He had commanded *Scharnhorst* and *Gneisenau*'s successful sortie into the Atlantic, often infuriating his subordinates by refusing to divulge his plans and by strictly adhering to his orders to avoid contact with enemy warships. Brave, competent, egotistical and remote, he must have been the last man a battleship captain would want on board to take strategic control of a voyage, and his refusal to consult or to inform others of his decisions was ultimately to prove disastrous. But he was no fool. He had warned Raeder that to undertake Rhine Exercise with only *Bismarck* and a cruiser was foolhardy. He said his final farewells to his friends before he left Germany, knowing that he was almost certain to lose his life in the operation. He obeyed his orders and accepted his fate.

Bismarck's captain, Lindemann, presents an altogether more attractive figure. A gunnery specialist, he insisted on the highest standards of efficiency and preparedness on his ship, but was at the same time a decent, humane leader and was highly esteemed by his officers and men. He was especially well regarded on the lower deck, where his aristocratic charm, good nature and unfailing fairness was deeply respected. His officers, too, found him very demanding but at the same time a polite, decent and above all highly competent chief. Unfortunately history records little about his relationship with Lutjens, but there are indications that the two clashed on several occasions. An admiral on board a ship is almost always bad news for the captain, but this seems to have been a particularly unhappy pairing.

On the British side, naval affairs were theoretically in the hands of Admiral of the Fleet Sir Dudley Pound. Pound had successfully commanded the battleship *Colossus* at the Battle of Jutland, and had risen steadily in the post-war Royal Navy. By 1941, however, he presents a rather sad figure, sick with what was to prove a fatal brain cancer, unable to sleep, and constantly trying to fight off the pugnacious and often down-right absurd interventions of Churchill, who regarded himself, with no justification whatever, as an expert in naval affairs. Not tough enough to fight Churchill, or fit enough to get his head properly around major issues, he resorted to trying to micro-manage naval operations, making bad decisions and infuriating or confusing his subordinates by sending them constant un-necessary signals. He also developed an unfortunate habit of accusing senior officers of cowardice and setting up courts of inquiry into their conduct. On at least one occasion this became so infuriating that it caused senior admirals to threaten to resign.

The senior commander at sea who played the major part in the battle was the C-in-C Home Fleet – Admiral Sir John Tovey. Tovey was one of the generation of British admirals who had graduated to the senior ranks through commanding destroyers in the First World War. Destroyers at that time were com-manded by lieutenants and lieutenant-commanders, and thus gave a new generation of naval officers a chance to operate independently, away from the stultifying conformity demanded in big ships. He proved himself a brave, dashing and successful destroyer captain. Deeply religious, he had a strong sense of what was right, and was determined and outspoken to the extent of being confrontational with anyone with whom he dis-agreed – even Churchill. Tovey was an excellent leader of men, always commanding happy ships and impressing his officers, not only with his professional competence, but also with his impish sense of humour and his good nature. Before taking command of the Home Fleet in 1941, Tovey had distinguished himself in action against superior Italian forces, leading a fleet of cruisers against heavy enemy ships, which soon turned away to avoid battle. Certainly mistakes were made during the hunt for *Bismarck*, and Tovey must bear some of the responsibility for some of them; nevertheless, he must rate as one of the finest British leaders of the war. His strength of character was well displayed soon after the *Bismarck* operation, when a senior officer under his command was threatened with court martial as a result of one of Pound's pathetic attempts to assert himself. 'If this is allowed to proceed,' he wrote to Pound, 'I shall resign my command and appear at the court in the role of defendant's friend.' Not another word was heard on the matter. What a man to have as your commander-in-chief.

Admiral Sir James Somerville commanded what was known as 'Force H', based at Gibraltar. Originally a signals specialist, Somerville, like Tovey, was extremely popular with his officers and comes across as a decent and inspirational leader. He was especially keen to improve the standards and performance of the air arm allotted to him, insisting on the aircrews of his carrier-based aircraft getting in a maximum of flying-time, constantly practising air defence and bombing runs. As a result, his aircraft were probably the most effective in the Royal Navy. He had already seen much action against the Italian fleet and had had the unpleasant job of destroying the French ships at Mers-el-Kebir. His protests at having to carry out this operation, which he considered unnecessary, won him no friends at the Admiralty. Perhaps this was why in July 1940 he found himself facing one of Pound's courts of inquiry after recalling his ships from a chase after the Italian fleet when it became clear that his precious carrier *Ark Royal* was in danger of attack from Italian shore-based bombers. The court cleared him, but the incident left a nasty taste. Force H had also been involved in the unsuccessful hunt for *Scharnhorst* and *Gneisenau* in the Atlantic, in escorting convoys through the Mediterranean, in flying off Hurricane fighters to Malta and in protecting convoys moving along the African and Iberian coast. Somerville was having an extremely active war.

It is interesting that both Tovey and Somerville were great jokers, often telling tales about themselves. Two examples:

Tovey (newly promoted to rear admiral, to newly recruited reserve seaman who had not saluted him): You! Why didn't you salute me?

Recruit: I'm awfully sorry, sir, I didn't see you.

Tovey: Do you know what these rings on my sleeve mean?

Recruit: Yes, sir, they mean you are the lowest form of admiral.

Tovey collapsed laughing and the recruit was excused.

Renown was Somerville's flagship. On one occasion her anti-torpedo armour came adrift and was projecting from her bows underwater. Some Swordfish from *Ark Royal* flew low, close to the bow, to inspect the damage.

Somerville to *Ark Royal*: Why are your aircraft doing that, expecting to see something sticking out of my pants?

Ark Royal to Somerville: Don't flatter yourself, it's dangling out, not sticking out!

Somerville roared with laughter.

It is difficult to imagine such exchanges between senior admirals of the Kriegsmarine.

No description of the *Bismarck* action can be complete without a brief examination of the intelligence operations undertaken by both sides. The German navy had been appalled after the First World War when they found out that British intelligence had been reading all its radio messages from December 1914 onwards. It determined to establish a completely secure system for the future, and the result of this was the famous Enigma machine – a device that scrambled messages by means of a series of gearwheels and random electrical connections. One of these devices was obtained by Polish intelligence before the war, and the Poles solved most of the problems concerned with reading the code. After the fall of Poland this expertise was moved first to France and then to Britain. Soon British intelligence was reading the simpler versions of the Enigma codes used by the *Luftwaffe* and the army, but the naval code was more difficult to crack, as an extra wheel was fitted to the machine, multiplying the problems several thousandfold. Also, the navy used a random system of designating grid references on charts, making it impossible to decipher position references without an up-to-date key document. By May 1941 naval Enigma messages could sometimes be read, but the process was slow and unreliable. This problem was about to be resolved when the Enigma machine and code books seized from U.110 by the destroyer *Bulldog* in early May became available to the decoding teams, but this was just too late to be useful in the *Bismarck* hunt.

At the same time as they were developing the Enigma procedures, the Germans made a detailed study of all that was known about British codes, and by 1939 they had cracked virtually all the British naval systems. This was a huge advantage, especially when planning U-boat and surface raider operations in the Atlantic, because it enabled the German commanders to know exactly when convoys set out and gave some indication of their progress. Also, on their capital ships, small *B-Dienst* (radio intelligence) teams were established, and these were expert at signal monitoring and code breaking, so that they could advise the ships' officers of enemy signals and intentions. The situation in May 1941 was therefore that the Germans were slightly ahead of Britain in the area of code breaking, but this position was about to be reversed.

Each side also used high-frequency direction finding to locate the source of the other's signals, but the British HFDF (Huffduff) locators were more widely installed, many of them on ships at sea, and these generally seem to have been more effective than the land-based German systems. In the field of physical intelligence, Britain had the enormous advantage of having patriotic spies based in occupied countries providing a constant stream of information. On the other hand the overall efficiency of German intelligence gathering by means of agents, photo reconnaissance and routine information collection was extraordinarily poor, in sharp contrast to most of their military operations. This was partly due to inter-service rivalry, but another reason was that the *Abwehr* military intelligence operation, run by Admiral Canaris, was never really trusted by Hitler and his cronies. It seems to have degenerated into a shambles.

Having examined very briefly the resources and the senior personnel available to both sides, we should return to the movements of those two massive ships stealing out of Gotenhaven.

CHAPTER 4

Goodbye to the Baltic

Bismarck and *Prinz Eugen*'s departure was none too early. Raeder had originally set 26 April as the date for the start of Rhine Exercise. The new moon would be giving little light, so movements were less likely to be observed by the enemy, and the nights in the high latitudes would still be long, helping to ensure a stealthy break out into the north Atlantic. Once there, there would be enough daylight to carry out successful attacks, and enough darkness to sneak away if enemy capital ships threatened. Various supply ships and tankers were ready to position themselves to sustain the warships at sea.

From a strategic point of view also, April would be a good time to divert British forces from the Mediterranean. This would allow the army to complete the rout of the Greek and British defenders of the last outposts on Greek territory and give Rommel a chance to continue his advances in north Africa with a minimum of interference from the Royal Navy and the Fleet Air Arm. Even more important in his view was the approach of the launch of Operation Barbarossa against Russia. The navy badly needed a major success story before news from the victorious armies on the Eastern front started to dominate the news.

Unfortunately for him there were seemingly endless delays. *Bismarck*'s aircraft crane malfunctioned and needed repair by the maker. A series of problems beset *Prinz Eugen*. An errant practice torpedo damaged a propeller. While in dock, having

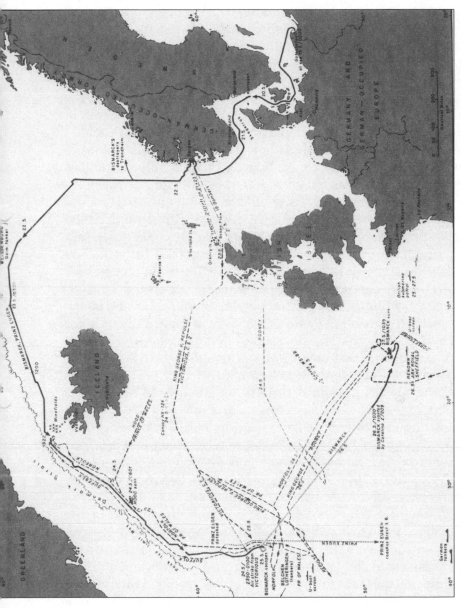

General view of the course of the major ships involved. Note the position of the tanker *Weissenburg* in the Arctic Sea, ideally placed to re-fuel the German ships during their outward voyage. This chart shows clearly how *Bismarck* could have found a shorter route back to Germany after the Battle of the Denmark Strait. Passing south of Iceland she would have risked an encounter with Tovey's main force but if she steamed back through the Denmark Strait she could have got under cover of German Norway-based aircraft before any heavy British ships could have got to her. Instead she chose the long haul towards the French ports.

this repaired, she was damaged by near-misses from RAF bombs, then worst of all she detonated a mine, also dropped by the RAF, a few metres off her bow, causing severe damage to her bottom. Repairs were rushed forward, but the operation had to be postponed. During the delay Lutjens was summoned to Berlin for a final briefing. He was instructed to make every effort to avoid action that might lead to damage to his ships. He was to use *Bismarck* to deal with the escorts, and *Prinz Eugen* should sink the transports. No attention should be paid to rescuing survivors. (This barbaric instruction would probably have been ignored by commanders at sea. German naval officers normally exhibited decent standards of humanity in combat situations. A little later than the *Bismarck* operation, Goebbels suggested that U-boat crews should machine-gun survivors of ships they torpedoed, so as to discourage British and Allied crews from joining the Merchant Navy. The *Kriegsmarine* rejected the idea out of hand.) If the ships were forced to fight they should do so 'with full force and to the finish'. In fact Raeder seems to have concocted a set of operational orders that covered his own position whatever happened, enabling him to blame the force commander if anything went wrong. Lutjens once again suggested that the operation should be delayed at least until one of the battleships in Brest could be ready to join in the venture, but Raeder was adamant. It was left to Lutjens to spend his last days in Berlin saying goodbye to his friends. On board *Bismarck* the last day in harbour was spent in the disgusting task of fuel bunker cleaning. Filthy oily sludge was scraped out from the tanks by Polish slave workers and dumped into barges alongside. This may have reminded some of the officers of the nature of the regime for which they were fighting. Everyone involved got covered in black oil.

Although secrecy was absolutely key to the success of the operation, this was compromised from the start by the ship's band, which played '*Muss I denn*', the traditional departure tune for warships as they moved away from their moorings.

Little did the Germans know it, but British naval intelligence already had an inkling that a sortie by the *Bismarck* was about to take place. An Enigma machine and related documents had been captured from an armed trawler near the Lofoten Islands a few weeks earlier. This small ship did not carry the full German naval encrypting equipment, but its up-to-date version of the codes and charts used by the *Luftwaffe* made it relatively easy to read messages relating to intense air reconnaissance over the Denmark Strait and asking for reports on ice conditions there. It was not difficult to conclude that a raid on Atlantic shipping by surface-ships was in the offing, and the only large surface ship ready to sortie from Germany was known to be *Bismarck*. Was this one of the frequent 'flaps' and false alarms that so often ran through the fleet at Scapa Flow? Perhaps, but preparations were set in hand and plans made for aerial reconnaissance.

The first leg of the voyage lasted less than an hour. The ships anchored in Gotenhafen Roads, where they took on some last-minute supplies and conducted further exercises. Most importantly, both ships took on oil. During this process a hose ruptured, preventing *Bismarck* from filling up completely. She therefore set out with only 7,000 tons, 1,000 short of her full capacity. At the time this did not seem to matter. They were to refuel in Norway, and in any case a veritable fleet of supply ships and tankers was lurking in obscure parts of the Arctic Sea and the north Atlantic to allow the warships to prolong their voyage for several months. Even with only 7,000 tons of oil her range was far greater than that of her consort, *Prinz Eugen*. At 0200 on 19 May, the voyage proper started. The two big ships, turbines gently rumbling below decks, nosed slowly out to sea. Around them three of Germany's now small stock of destroyers gave anti-submarine protection (British subs had operated in the Baltic early in the war), and ahead of them steamed a *Sperrbrecher*. This was a merchant ship, its hull reinforced with steel and concrete and having a very deep draft, which would sail ahead of valuable warships so as to set off any mines in their path. A *Sperrbrecher* would normally survive mine explosions with little damage. The fleet steered west through the Baltic and into the Great Belt – the network of islands between southern Sweden and Denmark. This area had been closed to commercial traffic to allow the warships to pass through unobserved. Officers on *Bismarck*, however, were alarmed to see so many fishing-boats. They knew that some of these might be in contact with British agents, and feared for their security. In fact it does not seem that any reports reached London from this source. The day dawned warm and sunny on 20 May, and as they steamed through the Kattegat the first serious alarm was sounded. One of the destroyers detected a strong force of aircraft approaching at high speed. Guns were manned, but the aircraft were recognised as friendly fighters, the *Luftwaffe* having failed to inform the navy of their intention to cover their passage. It was an ominous precedent, pointing to poor inter-service communication. A further problem arose early in the afternoon. A large warship was sighted steaming northwards along the Swedish coast. She was identified as the Swedish aircraft-carrying cruiser *Gotland*, returning from exercises off Vinga. Lutjens immediately feared that *Gotland* would report their presence to Stockholm, and thence the information would leak to the British. He signalled the admiral commanding the German northern sector, Rolf Carls, saying that he feared security was compromised. The reply he got was reassuring. 'No, Sweden is strictly neutral and will not pass information to Britain. There is little danger.'

The captain of *Gotland* was a Nazi sympathiser, but he duly reported *Bismarck* and *Prinz Eugen* to Stockholm, where it found its way to a naval intelligence officer, Lieutenant Ternberg. Like many Swedes, Ternberg was disgusted by the German invasion of Norway and Denmark, which he considered in the long term a danger to his own country. He had cultivated a relationship with a Colonel Lund, the military attaché in Stockholm of the Norwegian government-in-exile, now based in London. Lund in turn was a close colleague of the British naval attaché in Stockholm, Captain Henry Denham. Ternberg lost no time in letting Lund know *Gotland*'s news, and Lund in turn ran Denham to earth that same evening in a Stockholm restaurant. Realising the importance of the information, Denham leapt rather comically onto his bicycle and pedalled off to the embassy to send a top-priority secure telegram to London. Operation Rhine Exercise had been discovered. Denham's report confirmed the picture suggested by the intercepted *Luftwaffe* traffic, and it was now primarily a question of finding out exactly what the mission of the two ships was and what route they would follow. The aerial British reconnaissance over Norway was set in hand, and elements of the Home Fleet were alerted for action.

When the *Bismarck* operation had been successfully concluded, Denham received a signal from the Admiralty recognising his good work. It was the crowning glory of an otherwise unremarkable naval career.

Had Lutjens known about the information leak so early in the voyage, perhaps he would have returned to the Baltic, or at least decided to hole-up for a longish period in a Norwegian fjord. But he was misled by Carls's misplaced confidence in Sweden's goodwill, and persisted with his plans.

The afternoon of 20 May saw the convoy entering the minefields off the south of Norway, through which they were escorted by a minesweeping flotilla. To their dismay a large contingent of merchant ships, which had been waiting south of the minefield, tagged on behind them and subsequently followed them north. This further threatened security. Once through the minefield, the big ships accelerated to 17 knots and zigzagged to avoid submarines. This was perhaps the most peaceful part of the voyage, and crew members who were not on duty were able to relax and watch a film show. Many of them were young naval recruits, and this was their first long sea voyage. They had boundless confidence in their ship and in their captain, and were excited at the prospect of seeing action for the first time. Only the old hands who had served in the First World War knew what a ghastly affair a naval battle was for those involved, or understood anything of the risky nature of the enterprise on which they were engaged. The guns were manned at all times and a sharp lookout maintained for enemy submarines and aircraft. Later that evening speed was increased to 27 knots. The ships skirted a large minefield off Kristiansand, then turned west, and then north towards Bergen. Little did they know it, but keen eyes on the Norwegian coast were watching their progress. Viggo Axelsen, a resistance worker, saw the ships through binoculars from the mainland and got an immediate radio message through to London. A few minutes later another resistance member and keen bird watcher who was pursuing his hobby on Heroya Island nearby actually photographed the ships as they passed. He also got a message through. It is difficult after so many years to appreciate the courage it took for these patriots to defy the occupying army and risk sending radio messages to London. The occupiers had no shortage of radio detection gear, and capture would lead to the foulest torture and eventual death.

Early in the morning, the cliffs of the islands around Bergen came into view and the big ships anchored in the Grimstad-fjord, just south of Bergen, close to the shore. The rest of the day was spent painting the ship. They had had dazzle-paint stripes for their journey through the Baltic, but now they changed to standard battleship grey for the Atlantic. *Prinz Eugen* was refuelled from a tanker. For some unexplained reason *Bismarck* did not refuel, in spite of the fact that she had set out with her tanks less than full. It is true that the tanker *Weissenburg* was waiting for her north of Iceland, but it seems to have been madness not to have topped-up at every opportunity. As the ships rode at anchor in the fjord, an umbrella of fighters kept guard overhead. High above the fighters, however, another air-craft was operating unseen. A fast, unarmed, high-flying Spitfire belonging to RAF Coastal Command, and piloted by Flying Officer Suckling, had been dispatched to confirm Denham's report. Suckling's was one of three Spitfires that were searching the fjords on the Norwegian coast for any sign of large war-ships. Right at the end of his patrol he spotted *Bismarck* and *Prinz Eugen* in their hiding place. This was well away from the port of Bergen, in a steep fjord, close to the shore, where they had hoped to be difficult to spot. He circled and took some excellent pictures of the two ships. Close examination of the photos enabled the Admiralty to confirm the identity of the warships. Suckling had thought he had seen two cruisers, but his photos showed very clearly the true significance of his find.

Bismarck was out!

It is often questioned why Lutjens stopped off in Norway at all, and particularly why he chose to do so at a place so close to Britain as to be well within range of bombing and recon-naissance aircraft. If he felt he had to pause in his voyage to the north Atlantic, a northern port such as Narvik would have been much safer. He must have realised that stopping near Bergen endangered the security of the mission, and it seems to have served no useful purpose. It was certainly not called for in his operational orders. Baron von Mullenheim-Rechberg, the senior surviving officer of *Bismarck*, suggests that it was always his intention to stop in Norway if visibility off the Norwegian coast was good and therefore the British were likely to be able to track his voyage north. This does not seem a very good reason. The existence of the task force was much more likely to be betrayed by local resistance workers in Norway than by aircraft or submarines happening to come across it at sea. The pause in Norway was perhaps the first of Lutjens's catalogue of mistakes during the operation; the failure to refuel was the second.

Sometime that evening, *B-Dienst* on board *Bismarck* retrieved some disheartening information. A message to RAF units had been intercepted, instructing them to search for two large warships heading north up the Norwegian coast. Now it was clear even to *Bismarck*'s officers that the hunt for them was up and they could expect the full weight of the Royal Navy to be unleashed against them. They had no idea how the information had leaked out. Some blamed the Danish fishing boats and some *Gotland*. At 1930 hrs they raised anchor and, still with their destroyer escort, steamed northward into the night.

The hunt was indeed up. The Royal Navy knew quite a lot about *Bismarck*. Some of their knowledge was gleaned from aerial reconnaissance, and some from contacts in the Swedish navy, whose officers had visited the ship. It was very clear to Tovey, on board his flagship *King George V*, lying in Scapa Flow, that she would be more than a match for any single ship under his command. The first question facing him, once it was confirmed that she had reached Norwegian waters, was as to her mission. Here he was at first confused by the small fleet of merchantmen and tankers that had attached itself to the two warships as they steamed through the coastal minefields. Were the capital ships a strong convoy escort, and if so where was the convoy going? Maybe to invade Iceland. Maybe the Faeroes. Maybe to the Arctic islands of Svalbard. Perhaps to deliver supplies and troops to northern Norway, or for some reason to northern Russia. Possibly the warships were not a convoy escort at all but planned to stay in the fjords, ready to pounce on British ships anywhere north of Shetland. He could afford to ignore no possibilities, but he soon decided that by far the most likely destination was the north Atlantic and another commerce-raiding expedition. If this was the case what route would they take? There were several possibilities. The Shetland–Faeroe Gap was the most southerly route, but could probably be ruled out because of the proximity to Scapa Flow and to British air bases in Scotland. Another route was north of the Faeroes, between them and Iceland. This was the most direct route, and was in fact the course that Lutjens had been instructed to take in Berlin. There was another route north of Iceland, passing south of the deserted island of Jan Mayen, and then south-west through what is known as the Denmark Strait, skirting the ice shelf off Greenland to starboard and the rocky coast of Iceland to port. These remote waters were too distant for the British to patrol regularly with aircraft, and weather conditions there normally made them ideal for concealing even the largest warships. This was the route that Lutjens had taken previously with *Scharnhorst* and *Gneisenau*, and Tovey concluded that it was probably the one he would take again. The intercepted *Luftwaffe* traffic seemed to confirm this. However, he had to be careful to keep all his options open. The forces available to him were limited enough without sending any of them off on a wild goose chase. Ships dashing about the Atlantic would soon run short of fuel and so would have to return to port just when they were most wanted.

Tovey's fleet was already widely extended on convoy escort duties, but luckily he was able to withdraw some of the escorts and deploy them so that they could be ready to intercept *Bismarck*'s foray wherever it appeared in the North Atlantic. Two radar-equipped cruisers, *Norfolk* and *Suffolk*, were already patrolling the seas around Iceland. They were ordered to refuel immediately and get into position to patrol the area between the Greenland ice pack and a minefield that extended north-west from the north-westerly tip of Iceland. To intercept the enemy in, or close to, the Denmark Strait, the new battleship *Prince of Wales* and the battle cruiser *Hood* would set out immediately for Iceland to refuel and then take station at the southern entrance of the Denmark Strait. The cruisers *Birmingham* and *Manchester* would patrol the Faeroes–Iceland Gap, and Tovey himself would remain at Scapa with the main force, consisting of *King George V*, the aircraft carrier *Victorious*, the old battle cruiser *Repulse* and supporting cruisers. The powerful but slow battleship *Rodney* was at sea on the way to an overdue refit in the USA. She was loaded with spare parts and assorted items of deck cargo, so that she looked even odder than usual. Her machinery was in a bad way and was only kept going thanks to constant attention and running repairs by her engineering staff. She was engaged in escorting the liner *Britannic* in the eastern Atlantic, so she would be in a position to join Tovey at sea later. In reality these forces were much stronger on paper than they were in fact. *Hood*, as we have seen, was a relic of a spectacularly unsuccessful First World War class of ship, and *Repulse* was even older and less heavily armed. *Prince of Wales* had only been commissioned in January and was still suffering major mechanical defects, especially in regard to her main gun turrets. Interestingly *Tirpitz*, which had been commissioned at almost exactly the same time, did not enter active service until January 1942, having taken a year to complete a process that *Prince of Wales* had tried to achieve in four months. A team of experts from Vickers was working on *Prince of Wales*'s main armament when she set out on the *Bismarck* chase, but its progress was slow. She was certainly not ready for battle. *Victorious* was also brand-new, having only been commissioned two months earlier, and she only received her complement of aircraft on 21 May. She carried only a minuscule strike force – nine Swordfish and six Fulmar fighters. The rest of her hangar space was taken up by crated aircraft bound for the Middle East. Her aircrews were very green and inexperienced, and few of them had ever landed on a carrier – a hair-raising experience in itself – until the 21st, when they all successfully put down on their new home, *Victorious*. The venerable *Rodney* would have no chance of keeping pace with a battle involving modern warships, so it would be difficult to bring her artillery into the action. The only fully worked-up modern battleship was *King George V*, and as we have seen, she was slower than *Bismarck* and mounted 14-inch guns as against *Bismarck*'s 15-inch. Her main armament had been giving constant cause for concern due to mechanical problems, which were in fact never fully solved on the British 14-inch turret.

Tovey ordered his main force to raise steam for immediate departure but remain at Scapa until the enemy intentions became clearer. As soon as he knew for certain where *Bismarck* was headed he would put to sea to intercept her. In the meantime he correctly decided that there was no point in dashing about the Atlantic using up fuel that might be required for a high-speed chase later.

The question arose as to whether a bombing raid could be mounted against the ships in the fjord. Tovey asked if *Victorious*'s Swordfish could make a torpedo attack, but was told that in view of the inexperience of the crews it seemed unlikely to succeed. Instead, a raid by land-based bombers – Hudsons and Whitleys belonging to RAF Coastal Command – was mounted, but before it took off the weather took a hand. A deep depression forming over Iceland began to make its presence felt. Cloud covered the Norwegian coast and visibility was restricted, making the raid abortive. Only two bombers got anywhere near the destination, and these saw nothing and bombed blind through thick cloud. They made a lot of noise, but in fact, as we shall see, the enemy ships had already departed. (A full timetable of events relating to the operation is given on page 161.)

Tovey, waiting with steam-up at Scapa, still needed to know what the German ships were doing so as to get into a position to intercept them. Were they still at anchor in the fjord or had they left, and if so in which direction? The weather was now so bad that all RAF operations were halted. There seemed to be no way now of getting reliable information. A solution to Tovey's problem was provided from an unlikely quarter. The officer commanding the naval air station at Hatston, in Orkney, Captain Fancourt, suggested that one of the Martin Maryland aircraft used by his station as target tugs could reach Bergen, flying low over the sea, and take a look. These were naval aircraft, and, unlike the RAF, naval pilots were not banned from flying through the thick weather. Fancourt had on his staff one Commander Rotherham, a highly experienced navigator, who had learnt to fly over water in the earliest days and had developed an uncanny knack of estimating speed and drift by looking down at the sea. Fancourt was convinced that if anyone could find the enemy's lair in the fjord, Rotherham could. Furthermore, he insisted that he himself would fly the mission as second pilot, in spite of his rather exalted rank. It would be a hazardous flight. They were approaching a coast heavily defended by ack-ack and by fighter planes, in thick weather, and the land rose steeply from the sea, so that the smallest error in navigation would almost certainly lead to disaster. Rotherham decided to adopt what is sometimes called the 'deliberate error' system of navigation. That is to say, that the aircraft steered some distance off course, so that when it encountered the land there was no doubt as to which way it should turn to find its objective. He proposed flying towards an island some fifteen miles south of the fjord, finding that, then striking north. He suggested that in fact the bad visibility was in many ways an advantage. German gunners would be off their guard, and fighters would not be in the air. The flight was duly authorised, and at 16.30 hrs on 22 May the aircraft took off. It was captained by its regular pilot, Lieutenant Goddard, with Fancourt himself acting as second pilot. Rotherham wanted to stay low enough to be able to observe the sea at all times, but the pilot thought this too dangerous as the cloud base was only feet above the rough sea surface. Instead, he flew about 3,000 feet up, diving down from time to time to make observations. In the end the navigation was spot on, and they arrived over the island exactly on schedule. As they did so, visibility improved a little and they had no difficulty in finding Bergen and its fjords. Over the anchorage and Bergen harbour they were greeted by a hail of ack-ack fire. The pilot for some reason decided that the best response to this was to dive directly towards the guns, and did not pull out until they were only 200 feet above the town. They were hit, but not too severely, and flew up and down the fjords several times looking for ships. They saw none. An urgent signal had to be sent to Tovey in case they did not make it home. The aircraft's radio decided to malfunction at this point, and they failed to get through to Scapa or to Coastal Command on any of the normal channels. As a last resort they tried the radio channel used for the Maryland's normal target-towing duties. By some fluke this got through at far beyond the normal range, and a surprised air traffic controller at Hatston found himself receiving a top-priority, top-secret signal, which he duly passed on. In fact all went well on the return journey and the Maryland landed safely back at Hatston. The news that it brought was electrifying. Tovey and his fleet put to sea headed for mid-Atlantic. Churchill telephoned Roosevelt to ask for help in 'marking down' the quarry so that the Royal Navy could kill it. (In fact no effective help was provided.) *Suffolk* refuelled and sped to join *Norfolk* at the north end of the Greenland Strait. These two heavy cruisers were placed under command of Rear Admiral Wake-Walker in *Norfolk*. Somehow *Bismarck* must be found and destroyed. Tovey found time to acknowledge the work done by the Maryland's crew. He signalled them as follows: 'This skilful and determined reconnaissance is deserving of the highest praise, as is the initiative of Captain Fancourt in ordering it.'

In fact *Bismarck* and *Prinz Eugen* had left their anchorage almost twenty-four hours earlier, at about 19.30 hrs on 21 May, met up with their destroyer escort and steamed north into worsening weather. As they left they saw the flak on shore behind them opening up on the bombers that were vainly searching for them from above the clouds. The weather steadily deteriorated, giving them an invaluable cloak of invisibility. They reached the latitude of Trondheim and dismissed their destroyer escort. Now the two big ships were alone. It is worth considering for a moment what this really meant. Neither British, American, Japanese nor Italian capital ships normally operated at sea without a screen of destroyers to guard against submarines and provide an anti-aircraft picket. But Germany, thanks to the Norwegian operation and the battles of Narvik, had no destroyers to spare. Here were two of the most valuable ships of the German navy, unprotected, sailing into an ocean dominated by the Royal Navy and patrolled by aircraft of the RAF and the Fleet Air Arm. It was an absurdly high-risk mission, and the senior officers concerned – Lutjens, Lindemann and Brinkmann, captain of *Prinz Eugen* – certainly knew it.

Astonishingly, it was only at this point that Raeder informed Hitler that Operation Rhine Exercise had begun. The *Führer* had been told about it in principle when he had visited the ships in Kiel in spring, but he knew nothing of the timing. Then he had expressed doubts about the whole thing, pointing out, very wisely, the danger from carrier-borne aircraft, but Raeder had brushed this aside. Now that the operation was well under way without his blessing, Hitler was not best pleased. He demanded that the ships should be recalled if at all possible. Raeder said it was too late, and anyway the dangerous part of the voyage close to the British coast had been accomplished. To do it again in reverse would be even more risky. Grudgingly, the *Führer* concurred. He was probably more concerned with the mounting battle on and around Crete, where his magnificent paratroops were making progress, despite heavy losses, to pay much attention to what he regarded as a sideshow. 'But', he said, as he dismissed Raeder, 'I have a bad feeling about this.'

In the light of this, it is interesting to speculate again about Lutjens's real motives. He himself had openly challenged Raeder about the wisdom of using his capital ships 'in teaspoonfuls', as he put it. He wanted to wait until at least *Tirpitz* and one of the smaller battleships could join the operation and give it a real chance of success. Until these reinforcements were available, *Bismarck* in a Norwegian fjord would be a constant thorn in Britain's side, forcing her to withdraw forces from other theatres to protect any vessels moving in the area north of the Shetlands. (In fact this was the very strategy later adopted with *Tirpitz*.) There is no doubting Lutjens's personal bravery or discipline, but perhaps his stop-over in the fjord was planned so as to give Hitler time to find out about the mission and abort it. This would also explain the extraordinary failure to refuel when he had the chance. There is not a shred of evidence to support this theory, but it does help to explain some of the mistakes that otherwise have to be attributed to such an experienced and professional commander.

As the two ships steamed north, they received some encouraging news. *B-Dienst* confirmed that *Luftwaffe* reconnaissance over Scapa Flow had sighted four battleships still at anchor. It was therefore assumed that Tovey did not know of their escape from the fjord, and was still waiting to find out where they were headed. It is difficult to explain this *Luftwaffe* report, which was made after *Hood* and *Prince of Wales* had in fact put to sea. There is a suggestion that the Royal Navy was

using wooden dummy battleships to fool just such a reconnaissance. This does not seem to be supported by evidence.
There certainly *were* such dummy ships in existence, but none
of them seem to have been in Scapa at that time. Possibly
Luftwaffe was simply careless, mistaking a few light vessels for
battleships. Maybe it had been confused by the presence of
some old ships used as anti aircraft hulks. Certainly they did
not take photographs, as the weather was too thick, but relied
on simple visual observation. There was actually only one
battleship in Scapa at the time – *King George V*. There seems
to be no explanation except carelessness. If Lutjens had had
accurate information at this stage, possibly he would have
refuelled in the northern latitudes from a tanker. Then he
might have hidden there for a while, allowing the British to
dash about the Atlantic searching for him, using up fuel and
resources. When the hunt had died down he could safely
reappear to prey on the convoy routes. As it was, he pressed on
with his voyage.

There were now good reasons for moving as quickly
as possible. The meteorologist on *Bismarck* – a civilian, Dr
Externbrink – predicted that the weather in the Denmark Strait
was likely to clear, and if they wanted to enter it unobserved
they would have to move fast. He seems to have had difficulty
in explaining this to Lutjens, but eventually the big ships
increased speed to 27 kts. The weather was indeed thick, with
a moderate wind and visibility down to 500 yards or less.
Not wishing to use their radar, so as to minimise the risk of
detection, the ships had some problems in keeping in contact
while maintaining a safe distance apart. Eventually *Bismarck*
turned on her powerful stern searchlight, which penetrated
the murk, even in the perpetual daylight that prevailed so far
north. Up until late during the night of 22 May, Lutjens still
had the option of making for the Faeroes–Iceland passage that
Raeder had suggested he should take. Encouraged, however,
by the evidence that his breakout was still undetected, and by a
signal from the German northern command that U-boats were
having big successes attacking convoys south of Greenland, he
turned north-west, heading towards Jan Mayen island. There
was now a further chance to refuel. Close to Jan Mayen the

tanker *Weissenburg* was standing by for this very purpose. Lutjens did not make use of her. On this occasion it is easier to understand his decision not to fill his bunkers. He had no time to lose if he was going to avail himself of the British ignorance (as he supposed) of his breakout from the fjord, and to take advantage of the thick weather. Finding *Weissenburg* and then refuelling both ships from her would have involved a long delay, and perhaps even a breaking of radio silence. If Dr Externbrink was right the weather was soon going to clear. He must push on.

Almost at the same time as Lutjens made his turn to the north-west, Tovey and his force was putting to sea. *Hood* and *Prince of Wales* were steaming towards Iceland to refuel, and *Suffolk* had refuelled and joined *Norfolk* off the north-west tip of that island. The jaws of the trap were closing.

Pushing on was certainly what Lutjens did. In the still frozen Arctic sea the two ships forced their way at high speed through a soft crust of sea ice, which tinkled musically against the hulls. On *Prinz Eugen* a slight increase in vibration indicated that the ice had caused a problem. One of her propellers had suffered minor damage from the ice. This did not reduce her speed, but may well have contributed to problems that she encountered later. It was very cold, but the wind, now a north-easterly, blew at 20 to 30 knots, almost directly behind them, so the apparent wind on deck was deceptively light. Visibility was patchy. At one moment bright sun illuminated the ice, and the crews could see the mountains and glaciers of Iceland thirty miles away; at the next the haze or the intermittent snow squalls came in again, blotting out everything. To starboard the pristine icefields protecting the coast of Greenland presented the most amazing and beautiful panorama to the crew. Young seamen who had never before left German coastal waters gazed in awe at their surroundings. In places the ice formed itself into fantastic shapes, sometimes resembling the form of a ship, and there were frequent false alarms from the lookouts. The daylight was constant, but at this point the ships took the risk of switching on their radar sets, and the sonar operators listened attentively to their equipment, alert for any sign of hostile reconnaissance forces. Gun crews were closed up, ready for instant action. The channel between the minefields off Cape Nord, the north-west tip of Iceland, and the impassable ice around Greenland, was only a few miles wide, and if the enemy was waiting for them anywhere it would be here.

CHAPTER 5

The Plot Uncovered

At 19.22 hrs the alarm bells sounded. Radar and sonar had contacted a fast moving target about seven miles away to port. The vessel had been steaming towards them on the port bow, but she rapidly turned around and fell in astern on the port quarter. *B-Dienst* immediately picked up a transmission from nearby. It was the cruiser *Suffolk*, and she was reporting their course and position. An hour later another alarm. Quite close out of the mist emerged the form of another heavy cruiser – *Norfolk. Norfolk* was in fact the flagship of Rear Admiral Wake-Walker, in command of the force watching the Denmark Strait. He was dangerously close to the big guns of *Bismarck*, and she opened fire, letting off five salvoes from her 15-inch main armament. These were the first shots the great guns had fired in anger. No hits were scored, and Norfolk disappeared again into the mist, laying protective smoke. Soon she joined *Suffolk* shadowing from astern a safe distance off. It was in fact *Norfolk*'s contact report that reached the Admiralty first. Probably *Suffolk*'s transmitter was adversely effected by fog and damp. The great battleship's fire had narrowly missed its target, but the barrage did have one notable effect. It put *Bismarck*'s own fragile radar out of action. Now blind in the fog, Lutjens signalled to *Prinz Eugen* to overtake her and take the lead, guiding the task force with her still operational radar. This led to a little drama of its own. It should have been easy for *Prinz Eugen* to speed up and pull ahead, but somehow something went wrong with the

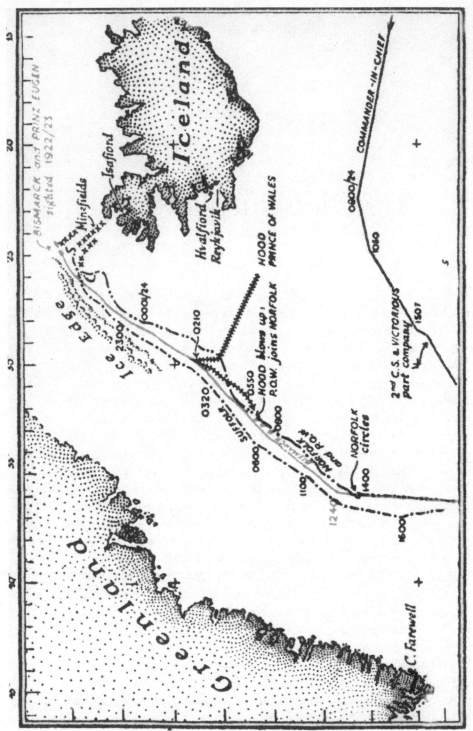

This chart shows the course of the ships at the time of the Battle of the Denmark Strait. Note how Admiral Holland's force trended too far north after radar contact was temporarily lost during the night, then had to turn south west and chase the German ships which had followed the ice pack and edged further to the west. Note that Tovey was not far away from *Bismarck* at this point. Had Holland simply joined the shadowing cruisers it might well have been possible for Tovey to have joined him so that they could have made a combined attack on the two German ships, assisted by *Victorious's* aircraft.

manoeuvre. Lindemann had left his bridge to talk to one of the gun crews when he got an urgent message from the officer of the watch. Looking out, he saw *Prinz Eugen* close at hand on a collision course. It is not easy to manoeuvre big ships close together at high speed – all sorts of strange proximity effects come into play. *Bismarck*'s skipper showed what he was made of. Giving the helm orders himself by telephone, he steered his ship out of trouble and *Prinz Eugen* safely took the lead. However, any satisfaction gained from observing the excellent seamanship of their captain was soon outweighed among the officers by the implication of their encounter with the cruisers. No more room for doubt. They had been identified and reported by the enemy. Sometime soon there would be a battle.

Suffolk herself had had an exciting time locating *Bismarck*. She had been cruising on a south-westerly course close to the minefields on the edge of the fog bank that obscured Iceland. Her radar could not search astern, so she had no advance warning of the great battleship that was rapidly overhauling her. An alert lookout, Able Seaman Newell, luckily spotted her, and Captain Ellis on the bridge immediately made a correct identification. She was only 14,000 yards away, easily within range, and it was a mercy that the German lookouts had not been as sharp-eyed as Newell, or *Suffolk* could have been blown clean out of the water. As it was, she dodged into the fog bank, let *Bismarck* pass, then commenced her radar-assisted pursuit.

Far away in London, the Admiralty team, with Churchill breathing down their necks, was making plans. There was an important troop convoy heading for Gibraltar, which would be severely threatened if *Bismarck* appeared in the Atlantic, and besides that there were ten other slow-moving convoys of freighters at sea. It was essential that these convoys, especially the troopers, should be protected effectively. The only force available to do this was Force H, based in Gibraltar and commanded by Admiral Sir James Somerville. He was immediately ordered to sea, with the primary task of protecting the troop convoy. Force H at that moment consisted of the old battle cruiser *Renown*, the aircraft carrier *Ark Royal*, and the cruisers *Sheffield* and *Dorsetshire*. *Dorsetshire* was temporarily detached on escort duty further south. *Renown* was even older than

Hood, and would be no match for *Bismarck*, but *Ark Royal* was a fairly modern carrier and her aircrews were some of the most experienced and best trained in the Fleet Air Arm, having gained plenty of battle experience in the Mediterranean. They were used to searching in the Atlantic also, having come within an ace of making a successful attack on *Scharnhorst* and *Gneisenau* during their Atlantic venture.

In the Denmark Strait there began one of the classic sea chases of history. Two great ships plunging forward, dodging whenever they could into the fog, and making smoke when there was none, racing south-west, at almost 30 knots. Behind them two cruisers keeping carefully out of gun range, but somehow maintaining contact and reporting regularly to Tovey. On each side of the four ships great fields of ice ranged, and behind the ice the huge, magnificent glaciers of Greenland occasionally appeared under the fitful sunlight. The sea in the Strait was moderate but the weather remained squally, and one squall caught *Suffolk*'s Walrus aircraft on its ramp and blew it clean over the side. Luckily no one was hurt, but no attempt could be made to recover it. Occasionally odd mirage effects occurred: once, when *Bismarck* was at the edge of a rain squall, the officers on *Suffolk*'s bridge saw that she had turned round and was headed directly towards them. They spun their ship round and fled northwards, only to find that the image disappeared. Also, their radar told them that *Bismarck* was still almost thirteen miles away on a steady course. Realising that they had been deceived by a trick of the light, they resumed their chase, steaming at full speed so as to keep within radar range. To the Germans the pursuit was uncanny. How could these cruisers know their every move as soon as they made it? What were the strange high-frequency pulses their own detector sets kept picking up? Surely the British had not got longer-range and more efficient radar than they themselves? That seemed the only possibility. Lutjens was intrigued. He must urgently inform Berlin of this alarming enemy capability, but at least there was one consolation. Their own receivers could detect the British signals. They could tell (at least he thought they could) when they were being observed.

Once, while she was hidden in a snow squall, *Bismarck* sprang a trap. Turning round, she rapidly closed the last known position of *Suffolk*, ready to blow her out of the water as soon as she appeared. But she did not appear. The Type 284 radar on Suffolk had warned her of the change of course, and she hightailed it north to keep out of range. *Bismarck*, not wishing to waste time and fuel, resumed her course. Soon afterwards, at about 00.30 hrs in a heavy snow storm, the radar pulses seemed to stop. Had *Suffolk* lost contact somehow? For almost three hours it seemed that she had, but then at about 03.00 hrs on 24 May the pulses started again: there seemed to be no escape.

Actually there had already been an escape, and perhaps a lucky one for the Germans. While radar contact had been temporally lost during the night, the two ships had altered course slightly so as to follow the line of the Greenland ice pack. As a result they had passed about ten miles ahead of a force of destroyers screening *Hood* and *Prince of Wales*, newly refuelled in Iceland and steaming to intercept. Had the alteration of course not happened, the destroyers would have spotted the two enemy ships, as visibility was three to five miles. Vice-Admiral Holland in *Hood* had hoped to meet his enemy in the semi-darkness and attack, using his destroyers and the *Norfolk* and *Suffolk* to divide the Germans' fire while *Hood* and *Prince of Wales* engaged with their heavy guns. His planned approach to the enemy was unconventional. He meant to attack more or less head-on, with *Hood* in the lead, steaming straight to meet *Bismarck* and *Prinz Eugen.* He thought this would bring down the range very quickly so that the vulnerable *Hood* would be exposed to the enemy's long-range plunging shells for the shortest possible time. Tovey was not happy with this idea, believing that it would be risky to allow *Hood* to take the lead. He pointed out that *Prince of Wales* was so much better armoured and could stand *Bismarck*'s fire with less risk of damage. He did not, however, order Holland to change his plan, believing that it was always better to let the man on the spot make the key decisions. There was another reason why *Prince of Wales* should have been in the lead. She was fitted with effective radar, which might have given her a decisive advantage in the opening stages of a long-range gun battle in poor visibility. Incredibly Holland ordered her to switch off her radar during the approach to the enemy 'so as to avoid danger of detection'.

As it was, everything went wrong with Holland's plan of attack. (The chart on page 58 shows the track of the various ships as *Bismarck* steamed down the Denmark Strait.) Firstly, as we have seen, the brief loss of radar contact by *Suffolk* and *Bismarck's* slight turn to the west caused him to steam past his enemy during the darkness. As soon as he realised that he had failed to find his foe he divided his forces, sending his destroyers off to search to the north, in case the Germans had turned back into the Denmark Strait, while his heavy ships searched to the west. An attempt was made to launch a Walrus spotter plane to help locate the enemy and watch the fall of shot, but the fuel was found to be contaminated and the plane had to be dumped over the side. Then, at about 03.00 hrs, *Suffolk* re-established radar contact. The new radar plot showed *Bismarck* to be some thirty-five miles away from *Hood*, tending gradually to the westward so that she was on a course almost parallel to her pursuers. This placed Holland at a severe dis-advantage. He would have to converge on his enemy from abeam, leaving his ships exposed to plunging fire for a longer period, and he would have to attack without any diversion caused by his destroyers, which were by now miles away to the north. To retain the possibility of taking his enemy unawares, he did not use his radio to give any orders to *Norfolk* and *Suffolk*, so that when the battle commenced they were too far away to be any help. The result of all this was that Holland went into battle with his forces divided and his heavy ships at a tactical disadvantage. He could, of course, have decided to follow the Germans without seeking battle and wait for Tovey to catch him up with *King George V*. This would have been a prudent course in view of the condition of *Prince of Wales* and the poor defensive armour of the aged *Hood*, but it seems that Holland never contemplated it. For him here was the one chance to prove that he was a fighting admiral in the old British tradition. Maybe he also believed in the mythical efficiency of the renowned 'mighty *Hood*'. He determined to offer battle immediately.

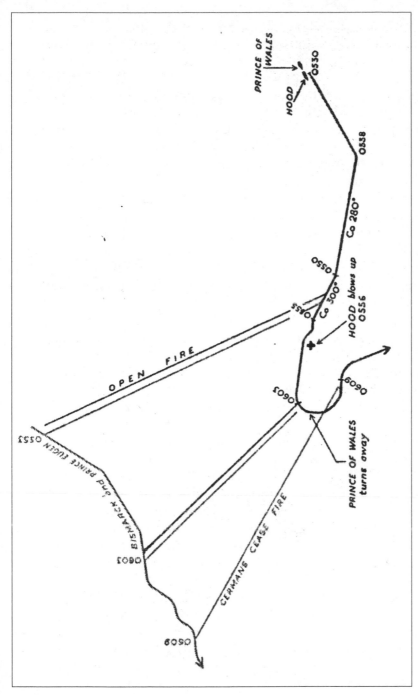

Movements of ships around the time of *Hood's* sinking. By altering course to port Lutjens was able to steer to cross Holland's tee. He could use the full broadside of both ships whereas Holland could only use his forward guns. *Hood* was turning to port so as to open her arcs of fire and bring her rear turrets to bear when she blew up. *Prince of Wales* had to dodge the wreck, then held her course for about seven minutes before turning away. Holland's approach angle was unfortunate as it allowed the Germans to dictate the course of the battle. It also resulted in exchanges of fire at long range which was extremely dangerous for *Hood* owing to her poor deck armour.

63

At 05.35 hrs a lookout on *Prince of Wales* spotted *Bismarck* about seventeen miles away. (A chart of this action is given on page 63.) They themselves had already been detected by German sonar, and were seen shortly afterwards. The Germans were still steaming on a generally southerly course with *Prinz Eugen* in the lead. They did not at first correctly identify the ships approaching them. They could not believe that a British battleship could be present, as they had been informed that *King George V* was still in Scapa, and they had no idea that *Prince of Wales* was in service at all. Were these cruisers? If so, how dare they approach in such an aggressive manner? Holland had ordered *Prince of Wales* to follow his movements exactly, so that Captain Leach had no scope for independent action. The two pairs of ships converged gradually, the British from slightly astern on the port beam of the Germans. It would thus be easy for Lutjens to make a turn to port ahead of them and cross Holland's tee. This he commenced to do. *Hood* opened fire at 05.52 hrs, with *Prince of Wales* following slightly later. Both ships had been ordered to concentrate their fire on the leading enemy, supposing it to be *Bismarck*. Leach realised the mistake almost immediately and switched to the rear ship. *Hood* soon followed suit. At first the British fire was ineffective. As they were approaching from behind, they could only use their forward turrets, so that eight of their eighteen heavy guns were out of action, while their opponents could employ their full broadsides. The situation was made even worse after the first salvo, when one of *Prince of Wales*'s guns failed. Another difficulty was that they were steaming into wind and sea, so that spray coming aft made it impossible to use the main rangefinders, which were mounted on the forward turrets. Instead they had to depend on the less-accurate instruments in the control towers. The Germans opened fire at 05.54 hrs. As usual they found the range quickly. At first both concentrated their fire on *Hood*, which by now had been correctly identified. There was tremendous excitement on board when they realised that they were now fighting the ship that they had so often used as an imaginary opponent, in real life. After only a minute a shell had struck some ready-to-use anti-aircraft ammunition, which was unwisely stored on *Hood*'s deck, starting a fierce fire. This shot probably came from *Prinz Eugen*, and another shell from the same source probably struck *Hood* at the base of the funnel. Holland now ordered a turn in succession to port, so that the aft guns could bear. Just as she was turning, a salvo from *Bismarck* straddled *Hood* amidships, and one, or perhaps two projectiles went crashing through her armour. It is impossible to know exactly what happened next, but examination of the wreck suggests that one shell penetrated the 4-inch magazine, and the blast from this passed through the fuel tanks and on to the 15-inch ammunition. A plume of smoke and flame burst from a point close to the main mast, and then a massive explosion blew the whole ship in half. The forward part floated for a few seconds, during which one of the guns actually fired (or seemed to fire) a final round, and then the whole massive wreck sank for ever. A shower of splinters rained down on *Prince of Wales*, half a mile astern, and Leach had to swerve to avoid running over the wreckage. A mighty cheer rang through *Bismarck* and it took some time for the officers to restore order. There was a brief panic when a sonar operator on *Prinz Eugen* reported hearing approaching torpedoes. If any were fired they must have come from *Hood*, as *Prince of Wales* had no torpedo tubes, but it is highly unlikely that any torpedoes were in fact used. Probably what the operator heard were the eerie sounds made by the great vessel breaking-up. Only three of her crew of 1,418 survived. None of them was able to give a full account of what had caused the disaster.

Some alternative theories have been suggested to explain the loss of *Hood*. Just possibly the anti-aircraft ammunition fire caused by *Prinz Eugen's* guns got badly out of control and somehow spread to magazines deep in the ship. Certainly it was a terrible risk to have that ammunition stored unprotected on deck, but it seems unlikely that it could have caused an explosion of the main magazines. Another theory is that a malfunction in one of *Hood's* own turrets caused a flash-back into the magazines. It is certain that there had been problems with the turrets on several occasions, and although precautions had been taken against the possibility of flash-back, in the heat of battle short-cuts may have been taken, leading to a dangerous situation. This seems unlikely. Certainly *Bismarck* was seen by both German and British observers to straddle *Hood* just as she was turning to port, and it is difficult to believe that a shell or shells from this salvo was not the cause of the disaster.

Prince of Wales was now the only British ship left in the action, and she received the fire of both the Germans. At the same time *Prinz Eugen* manoeuvred to try to launch a torpedo attack. *Prince of Wales* was struck four times by *Bismarck* and three by *Prinz Eugen*. One shell passed through the upper super-structure, killing several men on the compass and air defence platforms. Everyone on the bridge except Leach himself, one other officer and a signaller was killed. Another damaged the radar office, killing some of its occupants. Two of the fire-director towers were destroyed. An 8-inch shell from *Prinz Eugen* entered the secondary ammunition chamber and whizzed around, mercifully without exploding. Had it done so the ship would probably have shared the fate of *Hood*. A 15-inch round from *Bismarck* hit below the waterline, penetrated the hull and was eventually stopped by the anti-torpedo bulkhead. This also did not explode, but 400 tons of seawater flooded into the hull. The total effect of the damage done by enemy gunfire was serious but far from fatal. Another factor, however, was becoming equally threatening to the new battleship. One by one, the 14-inch guns ceased to operate properly. The Vickers team on board fought valiantly to restore them, but as the failures reduced available armament from ten to seven guns, Leach realised that to continue the action would be to sacrifice one of the only two modern battleships in the Royal Navy. He made smoke and broke off the action. At the same moment, one of the turrets came off its rotating ring-gear altogether and became totally useless. As Leach retired, a few rounds from another source splashed around *Bismarck*. *Norfolk* had crept up on her without orders and opened fire at long range. She was easily driven off and her fire was ineffective.

Observers were surprised at the failure of *Hood*, whose gunnery was supposed to have been excellent, to perform better on that day when her target was well within range. The gunnery officer of *Prince of Wales* noticed no shells at all from her land-ing anywhere near *Bismarck*. It appears that during the first part of the action *Hood* was firing ineffectively at *Prinz Eugen*, then tried to shift to *Bismarck*, but somehow confusion between the bridge and the director team prevented her from firing effectively. Possibly attention was distracted by the spectacular fire caused by the anti-aircraft rockets. Certainly her fire-director system seems to have performed very badly, in comparison with that of the other three ships involved.

Prince of Wales on the other hand had not fought in vain. While *Hood* had scored no hits at all, she had hit *Bismarck* three times with her 14-inch main armament. The watching cruisers had observed the enemy's funnel let out a tell-tale puff of smoke, indicating that a concussion had loosened soot deposited in the funnel. (Illustrations 1–4 show detailed plans of *Bismarck*, and indicate locations damaged by *Prince of Wales*'s shells.) The first hit passed clean through the bow section of the ship, damaging the bulkheads between compartments XX and XXI and XXI and XXII, leaving a five-foot-diameter hole in the starboard side of the ship and admitting 2,000 tons of seawater. It also damaged fuel tanks, valves and pumps in the forward part of the ship. The second struck beneath the armoured belt alongside compartment XIV and exploded against the internal torpedo bulkhead. The port turbo-generator room was put out of action and the port and auxiliary boiler rooms were damaged. The nearby condensers were also badly damaged, which created a potential problem with the boiler feed water and could have led to the shutting-down of two of the main boilers. This hit also ruptured several of the fuel storage tanks in the bottom of the ship, causing a serious oil leak. The third shell hit one of the ship's boats and passed on over the ship without exploding. The damage inflicted by the first hit was the most serious. Water flooding the fore part of the hull put a terrific strain on the remaining bulkheads when the ship was moving at speed, threatening to collapse them. Eventually they were shored up and matting placed over the holes in the hull, so that the ship could make about 28 knots, but another problem was more serious. A thousand tons of fuel oil was stored in the forward compartments, and it proved impossible to enter the pump room and repair the damage there. An attempt to access the fuel tanks from above also failed, and the engineer's department had to report to the captain that there was no way to access the vital fuel stored in the forward compartments. Water also continued to rise in the area around the generator room damaged by the second hit, and the generator had to be shut down. This did not matter too much as there was enough reserve capacity, but the ship was now listing nine degrees to port and was three degrees down by the bows. This was later partly corrected by counter-flooding. Lindemann's engineers suggested that they should slow the ship down and heel her over by flooding to bring the damaged parts of the hull out of the water and make a more satisfactory repair, but Lutjens refused permission for such a manoeuvre. He wanted to push on without delay.

The damage to *Bismarck* had no effect on her ability to fight, and *Prinz Eugen* was entirely undamaged and her radar was still working. The obvious course would have been for the two of them to find *Prince of Wales* and sink her. It had become clear that she was damaged and that her guns were not working properly: she would soon have been overwhelmed by the gunfire of *Bismarck*. This aspect of the so-called 'Battle of the Denmark Strait' remains a mystery. Why did Lutjens allow *Prince of Wales* to break off the action and escape? There appears to have been a fierce argument between him and Lindemann on this issue, Lindemann pressing the case for following-up on the victory over *Hood*. Lutjens was adamant that they should follow their orders strictly and avoid conflict with heavy enemy ships if at all possible. This seems a strange attitude to take, seeing that he had ignored so many orders already about the route he should take and where to refuel. The German ships had the upper hand, and surely no one would have criticised Lutjens for sinking another enemy battleship, as would almost certainly have been the case. Hitler himself was of this opinion; he could not understand Lutjens's action, and criticised it strongly at the time. It remains a mystery to this day. As it was, the officers of *Bismarck*, astonished as they were at the breaking-off of the action, had to content themselves with a champagne party to congratulate their gunnery officer on his good shooting and to discuss the magnificent performance of their fine ship.

Captain Leach of *Prince of Wales* was criticised at the time for 'abandoning *Hood*' and 'running away'. This is absurd; he fought his ship bravely and well, and disengaged because it was the right thing to do at the time. As we shall see, the damage he did to *Bismarck* effectively started her on a fatal course of action. He also continued to try to bring his damaged ship back into action as soon as a favourable opportunity arose. Nevertheless, such was the prestige of *Hood* that *Prince of Wales* and her captain became figures of contempt in the navy, especially on the lower deck. The role of the two cruisers *Norfolk* and *Suffolk* was also brought into question. Why did they not attack with their 8-inch guns and their torpedoes? The answer to this is simple: they had no orders to do so, and anyway they were much too far away to use torpedoes with any chance of success. They had been almost twenty miles astern of *Bismarck* when the action commenced, and it would have taken at least thirty minutes to get to within torpedo range. The action only lasted eleven minutes. In a naval gun action it is critical that not too many ships are firing at a single target at the same time, otherwise it is impossible for a gunnery officer to watch the fall of his shot and correct his aim. If they had fired on *Bismarck* without orders, Wake-Walker's ships would have been criticised for spoiling the aim of *Hood* and *Prince of Wales*. In fact, as we have seen, *Norfolk* did try to engage towards the end of the action after *Hood* had blown up, but drew off when *Prince of Wales* disengaged. The cruiser's job was to shadow the enemy ships, not to sink them, and so far they had done this admirably. The conduct of Holland is somewhat surprising. He was a gunnery expert and was regarded as one of the cleverest men in the Royal Navy, with a clear head and an excellent brain. Why did he handle his ships so badly in the battle? Why did he not take advantage of the radar available to him? Why did he divide his forces when they so obviously should have been concentrated? A brave man, he was lost with his ship, and the questions will remain unanswered.

Wake-Walker, as the senior officer present, immediately assumed command of *Prince of Wales*, as well as his two cruisers. It was clear to him that his new charge would be in no condition to fight for some time, for he had seen her heel over sharply as she disengaged from the action, and noticed that her gunfire was sporadic and becoming inaccurate. This was due to damage to the guns and turrets. For the time being she would have to keep company with the cruisers and try to repair some of the damage. There was to be no respite for the unfortunate Vickers civilians on board as they worked ceaselessly to restore the turrets, struggling with huge steel structures and mechanisms on a damaged ship in a rising sea.

While the officers of *Bismarck* were celebrating their victory and congratulating Schneider, the chief gunnery officer, on sinking the pride of the Royal Navy, Lutjens, solitary, uncommunicative and forbidding, was coming to a crucial decision. He was not yet fully aware of the extent of the damage to *Bismarck*, although he knew that she was leaking oil and he must have noticed her list to port and bow-down attitude. He lost no time in making up his mind. It was foolish to continue his commerce-raiding sortie now that the enemy was obviously throwing the whole weight of the Royal Navy at his two ships. He had already concluded from the performance of *Suffolk*'s radar that the British had a system that would make commerce raiding by surface-ships difficult or impossible in the future. Of more immediate importance, the enemy radar would make it very dangerous for him to refuel at sea from a tanker in the west Atlantic as he had intended. No, he must make immediately for the French ports for repairs, and join forces with *Scharnhorst* and *Gneisenau*.

Only an hour after the battle, he signalled the *Seekriegsleitung* (German Naval Command) to tell them of his success against *Hood* and his fateful decision to abandon his mission. Why was St Nazaire chosen in preference to Brest, where the other ships were in dock? There were two very good reasons. St Nazaire was further from air bases in England, and the fate of ships in dock at Brest suggested that it was best to make life for the RAF as difficult as possible. Also, St Nazaire had a dry-dock facility large enough to accommodate a ship as beamy as *Bismarck*. The same signal also stated his intention to detach *Prinz Eugen* to attack merchant vessels on her own. *Prinz Eugen* had not suffered a single hit during the battle, and appears to have caused severe damage to both British ships. It is most significant that this key signal was sent at such an early stage, before a full assessment of the damage was completed and before *Bismarck*'s own engineering team had had time to see what, if anything, could be done to put matters right. At midday *Bismarck* and *Prinz Eugen* changed course to south-by-east, towards the Brittany ports. Neither Lutjens nor any of his immediate staff survived the battle which was to come, and his war diary was lost in circumstances which we shall examine later, but it is interesting to speculate on what his real motives were. The stop-over in Norway, the refusal to refuel, the rejection of the plan to repair the hull, all point to the fact that he was looking for reasons (excuses perhaps) to abort the commerce-raiding mission. It is one of the principles of warfare that forces should be concentrated and not dispersed widely in 'teaspoonfuls', as he had put it to Raeder. Having failed in his attempt to give Hitler time to cancel his mission altogether, he may have formed the intention to cut his voyage short and join *Scharnhorst* and *Gneisenau* in the Brittany ports. Such a strong force of warships there would completely destroy Britain's ability to send convoys towards the Mediterranean except with a heavy battleship escort. It might even force the Royal Navy to abandon North Africa and Malta altogether, and thus *Bismarck* would achieve at least one of her objectives without further risk. This could be far more advantageous for Germany than the uncertain outcome of a commerce-raiding exercise in mid-Atlantic. The damage suffered at the hands of *Prince of Wales* gave him an excuse for doing what he had hoped to do. *Bismarck*'s officers were certainly astonished by the decisions of their admiral, and the hint of conflict between him and their much-respected captain punctured their elation at their recent victory. From now on they would be running for safety, not searching for victims.

There were, of course, other options open to the Germans. The most obvious was to return to Norway, which was about 600 miles closer than the French ports, and the passage through the Denmark Strait might still be shrouded in fog to hide their ships from aircraft. Alternatively they could make a dash back through the Faeroes–Iceland Gap to the Baltic. These options were probably rejected because Lutjens had no idea whatever where the British fleet was, and he seems to have lost confidence in his own intelligence operation to tell him. After all, *Hood* and *Prince of Wales* (which he probably thought was *King George V*) had appeared out of nowhere when intelligence had told him that his breakout had been undetected and that the heavy British ships were all still in Scapa only twelve hours earlier.

While damage control parties were at work on *Bismarck*, *Norfolk* and *Suffolk* resumed their shadowing role. They were joined by the damaged *Prince of Wales,* still striving furiously to get her 14-inch main armament back into working order. Only three of her ten guns were capable of being fired after the action with *Bismarck*, but she was still an effective fighting ship and she had modern centimetric radar. At one point Lutjens ordered *Prinz Eugen* to drop astern and see if *Bismarck* was still leaving a noticeable oil slick behind her. She was. Not only that, but the unwelcome sight of a Sunderland flying-boat, and then a Catalina, appeared over the stern, keeping well out of range of the formidable flak guns. The aircraft also noticed the telltale oil slick trailing behind the enemy battleship, and duly reported that she seemed to be damaged. (Unfortunately their radio report was not properly understood, and it was not until the Sunderland's crew had landed in Iceland and been debriefed, hours later, that the news of the oil slick reached Tovey. Had Tovey had this information earlier he might have realised that *Bismarck* was unlikely to continue her breakout attempt into the Atlantic.) The aircraft could do nothing to hurt *Bismarck*, but they showed that she was now under even closer observation.

The next task for Lutjens was to part company with *Prinz Eugen*, if possible unobserved by the watchers. *Prinz Eugen* by herself would be more than capable of wreaking havoc among a lightly protected convoy, but she would have to be careful to avoid a clash with the many British capital ships converging on their position. Luckily the weather was now deteriorating rapidly, with dense patches of mist and heavy showers. After one false start, *Prinz Eugen*'s separation was accomplished at about 15.40 hrs. She at first held her course south-east while *Bismarck* turned sharply to starboard, to bring herself on a westerly heading, then completed her circle and resumed her former course, while *Prinz Eugen* slipped away to the south. Helped by a heavy squall, the manoeuvre was completely successful, although it brought *Bismarck* closer than she liked to *Suffolk*, who had to be driven off with salvoes from the aft turrets.

Suffolk's answering barrage was soon joined by the heavy gun-fire of *Prince of Wales*, which opened up on *Bismarck* at extreme range. The rough sea and deteriorating visibility made accurate shooting impossible, and no serious damage was done to either side. There was one exception, however. Perversely, *Suffolk* was damaged by her own gunfire. Her 8-inch forward guns, fired at high elevation, blasted back onto her bridge, shattering the steam-heated windscreen that had recently been fitted to equip her for service in Arctic waters. From then on, anyone on the bridge was subject to the full force of the bitter wind, making observation and communication doubly difficult. It is difficult to imagine how stressful and tiring it must have been to stand watch on that icy, windswept bridge, and this may partly explain some subsequent events. After this episode Wake-Walker ordered his ships to steam in line ahead, not as previously, with one cruiser on each quarter of *Bismarck. Suffolk* with her invaluable radar initially led, with *Prince of Wales* in the middle and *Norfolk* bringing up the rear.

It is appropriate here to follow the conclusion of *Prinz Eugen's* exploits. She refuelled from a tanker and headed for the south Atlantic to prey on unescorted shipping. However, the notoriously unreliable main engines soon gave trouble, possibly made worse by the damaged propeller. She was forced to turn round and make for Brest, where she became another target for RAF bombers. To avoid their attentions she eventually took part in the famous 'Channel Dash', but was then torpedoed by a British submarine, suffering heavy damage. She spent the rest of the war, unspectacularly, in German waters. After the war she was handed over to the US Navy and used as a target ship for atomic bomb testing at the Bikini Atoll.

On board *Bismarck*, it now became critical to eke out what fuel remained. Engineering staff had reported to Lindemann that there was no way of either stopping the leak in the bottom tanks or recovering much of the oil in the forward compart-ment. Speed was reduced to 22 knots to reduce consumption. A patrol of U-boats was ordered across her likely path towards the Bay of Biscay in the hope of trapping some of her pursuers. There could be no doubt that the British would by now have a formidable force trying to intercept her. Once she was within range of shore-based friendly aircraft, there was a reasonable hope of a safe arrival in France, but there was still some 1,000 miles – two-days' steaming – to do before she could hope for effective air cover.

The sinking of *Hood* had certainly stirred up a hornet's nest in the Admiralty. Almost every heavy ship in the north Atlantic was converging on the German intruders. Tovey with *King George V*, *Repulse* and the carrier *Victorious* were now almost within striking distance, but they still were not fast enough to hope to intercept her course. Tovey had been unsure of the German's intentions, and had steered roughly into mid-Atlantic so as to be best placed to intercept *Bismarck* whatever action she took. This led him by mid-afternoon on 24 May into a position about 200 miles east of his quarry, which was now steering more of less due south. He had not got the speed to intercept, but there were other possibilities. Force H from Gibraltar was steaming north into the Bay of Biscay area, and perhaps most important of all, the powerful battleship *Rodney* had abandoned the liner which she was escorting to the USA, and was making her best speed into mid-Atlantic to join the fray. The ancient battleships *Ramillies*, on escort duty in the west Atlantic, and *Revenge*, stationed in Halifax, Nova Scotia, were readied to attempt to intercept should the enemy try to break out south or westward. This was a fairly tall order considering that *Bismarck* was almost ten knots faster than they were. Very gradually, however, *Suffolk*'s reports of the enemy course made it more evident that he was heading south towards the French ports, or just possibly Spain or Gibraltar, and not to the west or back towards Germany by any of the northern routes.

CHAPTER 6

The Fleet Air Arm Takes
a Hand

To try to slow the enemy down and bring him to battle, Tovey now decided to detach *Victorious*, which was a much faster ship than *King George V*, and sent her on ahead at high speed to launch an attack with her aircraft. This was exactly the situation which Hitler had expressed concern about before the voyage – attack by enemy carrier aircraft when out of reach of friendly air cover. *Victorious*, it will be recalled, was a newly commissioned ship and her crew was inexperienced. There was some difficulty in keeping her engines operating efficiently and in keeping station with her escorts as she raced towards a point within range of *Bismarck*'s position, so that she could launch her aircraft. Her captain, Bovell, was continually concerned that his very green watch-keeping officers would make some mistake, leading to a collision or some other disaster. He himself had to be almost constantly on watch. *Victorious* was escorted by a small contingent of cruisers. It had been hoped to get within a hundred miles of the enemy before launching the attack, but the weather was deteriorating, so Bovell decided to launch while he was still 120 miles away. The Swordfish and the Fulmar fighters were ranged on deck, and at about 23.30 hrs the carrier turned north-westward into wind, and one by one they took off into the twilight. Although it was nearly midnight, there was still enough light to see, and the weather was partly overcast with a fresh wind and a rising sea, giving warning of the much worse weather that was to come. Nine Swordfish from 825 squadron took off without too much difficulty and formed-up on their leader, Acting Lieutenant-Commander Eugene Esmonde. Esmonde, in contrast to his fellow flyers, was a highly experienced pilot who had joined the RAF in 1925 on a five-year commission, most of which was served in the Mediterranean. He had then joined Imperial Airways, with whom he helped to pioneer the first airmail service between London and Australia. In 1939 he returned to service life, this time in the Fleet Air Arm. He had been waiting to take off from the carrier *Courageous* when she was torpedoed by U-29, and was lucky to survive. On *Victorious* he found himself leader of a group of newly trained aircrews, and he was practically the only experienced carrier hand on board. This did not bode well for a long-distance strike carried out against a powerful ship in deteriorating weather and with darkness falling.

The aircraft could only make some 85 knots into the prevailing headwind, but directed by *Suffolk*'s radar fixes and then by the ASV (air-to-surface-vessel) radars in the leading Swordfish, they found their target, only to lose her again in a particularly thick rain squall. Esmonde led his flight back to where he could communicate by signal lamp with *Norfolk*, got a revised heading and prepared to launch his attack. Firing a torpedo from an aircraft is no easy matter. The target should be approached through cloud if possible so as to minimise the time during which the aircraft is exposed to defensive fire. The next step is to dive down sharply from cruising height to 90–100 feet above the water. The weapon won't work at all if it is dropped too high or too fast or if the nose of the aircraft is not in the correct, slightly upward, attitude. This will allow the torpedo to enter the water at an angle of between fourteen and twenty-four degrees. Any deviation from this would cause it to dive to the bottom or bounce on the surface. Approach speed of 70–90 knots and from not more than 50 feet altitude was normal, but Swordfish pilots, because of the superb low-speed handling characteristics of their aircraft, often dropped from even lower than this. The aircraft must be flying straight and level at the time of the drop, and the range from the target should be between 500 and

1,000 yards. It is no good getting any closer than 500 yards, as the torpedo takes about thirty seconds after hitting the water to arm its fuse mechanism. The 18-inch Mark IX torpedo only travelled at a little over 30 knots, and so at 1,000 yards it would take a minute or so to reach its target. It is unlikely that the target ship would continue to steam on a steady course and wait for the torpedo to hit her. She would weave and swerve, trying to comb the track of the torpedo, while the attacking forces would make things as confusing as possible for her by approaching from several different directions. A Swordfish had a primitive sort of torpedo sight consisting of a metal bar with a row of lamps in front of the windscreen. When the pilot had estimated the speed of the target one of the lamps would be lit and he would try to line up the ship's bow with the illuminated lamp in line with the nose of the aircraft. This was a primitive system, and in reality it was mostly a question of having a good eye, a steady nerve and a lot of luck. The torpedo itself was not a particularly effective weapon. The British 18-inch torpedo was unlikely to damage a capital ship severely unless it struck a vulnerable point unprotected by anti-torpedo armour, possibly in the bow section or close to the propellers. This was the out-come, of course, of British neglect of naval aviation during the inter-war period. American and Japanese air-launched torpedoes were far bigger and more effective.

The inexperienced crews of 825 Squadron certainly showed no lack of nerve as they launched their attack. Several could not line up correctly on the first attempt, and came round again through the defensive fire to try again. The pilots, fresh from operational training school, had to skim low over the water, but the waves were high – up to twenty feet – and there was the constant danger of hitting the surface. Gunners on *Bismarck* reckoned their height at only six to twelve feet and that they approached to 400–500 yards before releasing their torpedoes. From each side of the great ship a storm of deadly missiles searched for the frail incoming aircraft. A single hit from the 5.9-inch secondary armament or the 4.1-inch anti-aircraft guns would have been fatal, and into the bargain the 15-inch main armament fired salvo after salvo into the sea in front of the attackers in the hope that the wall of water thrown up by the explosions would smash the Swordfish to pieces. The turbulence created by the heavy gunfire might also deflect torpedoes. As the aircraft got close enough to aim their missiles, a further barrage of fire from the 1.5-inch and 0.75-inch quick firers greeted them. Luckily many of these passed harmlessly through the fabric covering of the wings and fuselages. In spite of all these horrors the Fleet Air Arm pilots pressed on against their formidable adversary.

Victorious carried Fulmar fighters as well as her Swordfish. The Fulmar was a modern-looking two-seat machine with a 1,000 hp Rolls-Royce Merlin engine. It was much faster and more powerful than the Swordfish. Although too slow and clumsy to contend with land-based fighters, Fulmars were very rugged and had achieved some notable successes against Italian forces. During bombing or torpedo attacks they frequently gave air cover to Swordfish and at the same time diverted the attention of the enemy gunners. On this occasion, however, they seem to have achieved very little, due to the inexperience of their scratch crews. Few of them even got a glimpse of the target, and two became completely lost and ditched into the sea. Amazingly, one of these two crews was saved by a passing merchant ship.

On board *Bismarck* the observers simply couldn't believe what they were seeing – antiquated-looking biplanes, flying so slowly that their directors could not track them, staggering on through all their own gunners could throw at them. They seemed to come so close that they must ram the ship, but the defenders underestimated the tight turning-circle of the Sword-fish, and they all zigzagged away at low level. On the bridge the helmsman and the captain watched each plane as it came in and turned sharply towards it to avoid the torpedoes. In spite of the danger to the vessel's damaged structure, the ship built up speed to 27 knots. Suddenly a sharp explosion echoed through her. A hit! One Swordfish, approaching out of the setting sun, had got through, and his weapon struck *Bismarck* amidships, the explosion seeming to thrust the whole mighty vessel side-ways. Very soon the extent of the damage became clear. The torpedo had hit the heavily armoured centre section of the ship below the waterline, and several seamen in that area of the ship had been thrown off their feet, one being killed – *Bismarck*'s first fatality. There was no serious structural damage. The Mark IX torpedo only had a 250 lb warhead, puny compared to the 750 lb warhead of the Mark VIII 21-inch weapon used by submarines. Some of the matting that had been used to plug holes in the hull had been displaced by the violent manoeuvring, and the gash in the hull caused by the second shell strike had opened a little, letting in more seawater, but that was all. *Bismarck* was made of strong stuff. It was announced that at least five aircraft had been shot down, but the Germans were confused by their own gun splashes. All nine Swordfish survived the attack. They managed to stagger back to *Victorious*, guided partly by ASV radar and partly by a searchlight shining vertically from her deck. They all landed on safely – no small achievement in the dark on a deck heaving in the rising gale. For most of the pilots this was only their second deck landing. The searchlight had caused some controversy between Bovell and the commander of the escorting cruisers, Rear Admiral Curteis. Bovell was aware that his ship's homing beacon was out of order, and was extremely concerned for the safety of his flight crews. Well he might be, as it was now pitch-dark, blowing hard and raining heavily. Curteis, however, demanded that the light should be switched off, as it might attract the attention of U-boats. Bovell flatly refused, and a serious confrontation was only avoided by the drone of the engines of the returning aircraft.

Soon after the Swordfish started for home, *Prince of Wales* appeared out of the murk close behind *Bismarck* and opened up again with her 14-inch main armament. *Bismarck* replied, but once again no damage was done, and darkness called an end to the action. Shortly afterwards another target appeared on the starboard beam of *Prince of Wales*, and she came close to opening fire before it vanished again into a rain squall. It was lucky it did disappear, as the vessel was the US Coastguard cutter *Modoc*, which had somehow got herself between *Bismarck* and her pursuers. *Modoc*'s mission had been to reconnoitre the Greenland coast, but she seems to have been diverted towards the battle area. As a neutral ship she could play no part at all except perhaps to pick up survivors, and she seems not to have communicated with either side.

On *Bismarck* the effect of the air attack was actually to raise morale. The British had thrown first the mighty *Hood* at them, together with their newest battleship, and now the dreaded carrier aircraft had attacked, and yet there was still no serious damage. Surely nothing now could stop them reaching the French coast and the sheltering umbrella of the *Luftwaffe*? Alone in the admiral's quarters, Lutjens was more realistic. The air strike meant that British battleships could not be far away, and they knew his position and continued to track his every move. Sometime soon there would be an attack in force by surface ships, and there would be too many of them for even *Bismarck* to resist. Somehow he must escape from the watching radar on *Suffolk*, and find a way of evading his pursuers.

On *King George V* Tovey also expected an encounter sometime soon, probably on 25 May. He had no idea how badly *Bismarck* had been damaged, but he knew from Wake-Walker's reports that she had slowed down. He also by now had the Sunderland's report of the oil slick. He could not communicate with Wake-Walker because he needed to preserve radio silence, but it seemed that the two cruisers and *Prince of Wales* were driving the enemy southwards towards his track. *Repulse* was lightly armoured, but *King George V* was well protected, and he could expect the damaged *Prince of Wales* to join the action. Surely two British battleships, a battle cruiser and two heavy cruisers would be enough to finish the job? It would have been good to wait for the 16-inch guns of *Rodney* to make certain of victory, but she was still far away to the south and would probably be too late to join the battle. Tovey expected to be able to manage without her. In any case he could not postpone battle for long. He had been steaming at high speed for two days, and the fuel supply issue was becoming significant: he must retain enough to chase and fight his enemy and return as fast as possible to Scapa. He had no more than a day's supply in hand. But just as he was planning exactly where to approach his foe, a devastating message came in from *Suffolk*. *Bismarck* had been lost. There was no radar contact.

What had actually happened was this. *Suffolk* had been steaming off *Bismarck*'s port quarter, but she had been ordered to zigzag to avoid the danger of a U-boat attack. In fact a U-boat warning had just been issued by the Admiralty. To make things more difficult for the radar operators, she was further away from *Bismarck* than her captain would have liked because the Admiralty had pressed Wake-Walker to move *Prince of Wales* into a position from which she could creep up on the enemy and engage her from astern. *Prince of Wales* had therefore pulled ahead of *Suffolk* and was directly astern of *Bismarck*. This was an absurd idea, because *Prince of Wales* was not fast enough to get close if *Bismarck* chose to open the range, and even if she did so, it seems unlikely that she could engage such a formidable enemy successfully. All the move achieved was to force *Suffolk* to draw back nearer to the limits of her radar range. The cunning Lutjens had observed that *Suffolk* was zigzagging and opening the range, and planned to make use of it. In the darkness, at 03.00 hrs on 25 May, he waited until *Suffolk*'s zigzag took her to the farthest point from her quarry, just outside radar range, and then turned *Bismarck* to starboard, increasing speed to 27 knots. He then turned in a large circle, eventually settling on a course of south-east – directly towards St Nazaire. The plan worked perfectly, and radar contact was lost completely. There was one catch, however – radar works by sending out a pulse of radio waves that bounce off the target, and the returning waves are picked up by a receiver. *Bismarck*'s own main radar had been out of action since her first encounter with the cruisers, but she had another device, a radar detector, which told the operator when a pulse of enemy radar waves reached the ship, giving their frequency and an approximate bearing to their source. Unfortunately for *Bismarck*, the detector continued to pick up *Suffolk*'s signals long after the returning echoes were too weak to be detected by *Suffolk* herself. Lutjens therefore believed that he was still under observation when he had in fact got outside radar range. He had escaped but he did not realise it. (The disposition of ships involved and the positions plotted is given in the chart on page 82.)

The shadowing cruisers thought it likely that their quarry had slipped away to the west or south-west, perhaps to meet up with an oiler, and concentrated their searches in that direction, but naturally found nothing. *Victorious* flew off searches as soon as visibility allowed in the same direction, and was also

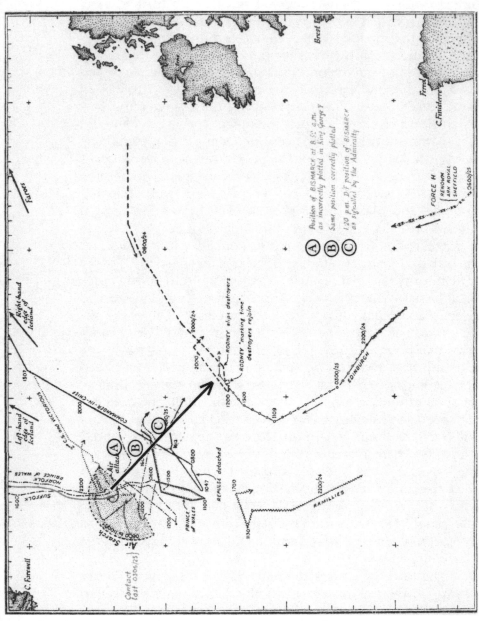

The loss of contact. After radar contact was lost *Bismarck*'s ill advised radio signals should have given her position away, but the incorrect plot caused Tovey to turn to the north east, on the assumption that she was making for home via the Iceland Faroes gap. *Rodney*, defying orders, marked time, having correctly guessed the enemy's true destination. By 13.20 the Admiralty had correctly plotted *Bismarck*'s track. Tovey, totally confused by the conflicting information he was presented with, at first steers east, then the correct course – south east.

frustrated. Tovey, keeping his options open, continued to steam westwards, towards mid-Atlantic.

Thinking that he was still under observation, Lutjens then made the mistake of sending two radio messages, unaware that these would reveal his position to the enemy. The first sent out at 07.00 simply stated, erroneously, that he was still being shadowed by the British cruisers, while the second, sent two hours later, was an extraordinary missive:

> Presence of radar on enemy vessels, with a range of at least 35,000 metres [actually it was about 24,000 metres] has strong adverse effect on operations in Atlantic. Ships were located in Denmark Strait in thick fog and could never again break contact. Attempts to break contact unsuccessful in despite most favourable weather conditions. Refuelling in general no longer possible, unless high speed enables me to disengage. Running fight between 20,800 and 18,000 metres ... Hood destroyed by explosion in five minutes, then changed target to King George V [Actually it was Prince of Wales], which after clearly observed hit turned away making smoke and was out of sight for several hours. Own ammunition expenditure 93 shells. Thereafter King George V accepted action only at very long range. Bismarck hit twice by King George V. One of them below side armour compartments XIII–XIV. Hit in compartments XX and XXI reduced speed and caused ship to settle a degree and effective loss of oil in compartments. Detachment of Prinz Eugen made possible by battleship engaging cruiser and battleship in fog. Own radar subject to disturbance, especially from firing.

The message told Naval Group West almost nothing they did not already know, but it was a heaven-sent gift to the British. It was long enough to give an excellent fix to radio direction finders, which fairly accurately plotted *Bismarck*'s position. In combination with the earlier message, it enabled Admiralty planners to get a very good estimate of her course also, so that it was becoming obvious that she was bound for the French coast.

They could not de-code the message, but its very existence told them all they needed to know.

Why did Lutjens, normally so uncommunicative, send these messages? True, he probably still suspected that he was being tracked by *Suffolk*'s radar, but he had been signalled during the morning by the naval HQ in Paris with the information that *Suffolk* had ceased sending position reports to the British Admiralty, and therefore it seemed likely that she had lost contact. His own signals intelligence staff probably gave him the same information. In fact *Suffolk*'s radar pulses must have been so weak by dawn, due to the long distance between her and *Bismarck*, that the operator of the detector himself must have doubted that contact was being maintained. Lutjens must surely have surmised from this that there was at least a chance that he had shaken off the British radars, and in these circumstances it was madness to break radio silence for non-essential messages. Neither he nor any of his staff survived the battle that was to come, so the answer will never be known. It has been suggested that strain, a fierce argument with Captain Lindemann over his refusal to finish off the wounded *Prince of Wales* and general pessimism about the outcome of the operation drove Lutjens into a temporary fit of irrationality. Another possibility is that he anticipated accusations of cowardice when he returned to port after failing to complete his mission, and he wanted to get his defence on the table as early as he could. Clearly he was extremely shaken by the efficiency of British radar, having previously believed that Germany was ahead of the game in this branch of technology. He was probably right in concluding that radar made the future of surface raiders dubious, but this opinion did not warrant a signal that might be fatal to his whole enterprise.

Astonishingly, however, it wasn't fatal. The Admiralty picked up Lutjens's message and duly transmitted the bearings to Tovey. Tovey had no way of checking them because his two HFDF-equipped (high-frequency direction-finding) destroyers were either out of action or refuelling. Unfortunately, Tovey's staff mistook the bearing sent to them from London, thinking it was a bearing *to* the transmitter when in fact it was a bearing *from* it. As a result they concluded that *Bismarck* was steering north-east, on a course back to Germany or Norway, not south-east towards France. (The chart on page 82 illustrates this.) As a result his force steamed past *Bismarck* going in approximately the opposite direction at a range of about a hundred miles. The air search mounted by *Victorious*'s Swordfish was also directed to the north-east, and naturally found nothing. The faithful *Suffolk* was also ordered to continue to patrol in a westerly direction to try to re-establish radar contact. As a result of this gaffe, only one large British warship remained between *Bismarck* and her destination – the 16-inch battleship *Rodney*, slow but formidable. She was, it will be remembered, on escort duty, looking after the liner *Majestic* bound for the USA. She was ordered to hand over her charge to the old battleship *Ramillies* – a First World War survivor even slower than herself – and join the hunt for *Bismarck*. At first she steered to intercept her quarry on the assumption that she was on a course for France, then a further signal came telling her to conform to Tovey's movements and steer north-east. Her captain, Dalrymple-Hamilton, was convinced, however, that this was wrong, and bravely ignored the order. He had formed a little committee of his own, consisting of himself, an American lieutenant commander who was travelling with him as a passenger, and his own senior and most trusted officers. This committee was convinced that the enemy was making for a west Atlantic port, either in France or Spain (Spain, though neutral, would probably offer repair facilities to a German warship, just as the USA was doing the same thing for the British). Dalrymple-Hamilton was determined that *Rodney* should be in at the kill. He staked his career on his own judgement. The other major British unit involved in the chase, Sommerville's Force II, was still steaming up the Spanish coast, its mission being primarily to give cover to convoys in the eastern Atlantic should any of the powerful German ships in Brest venture out. It seemed that the confusion as regards the bearings transmitted to Tovey might finally let *Bismarck* off the hook.

Gradually, however, evidence began to mount in favour of France as the German's destination. One element was a signal from a *Luftwaffe* general, Jeschonnek, whose son was a midshipman on *Bismarck*. He signalled from Athens, where he was overseeing the crushing defeat of British forces in Crete, asking *Luftwaffe* HQ where his son's ship was heading. HQ replied 'Brest' (actually it was St Nazaire). These signals in the *Luftwaffe* Enigma code were easily read by the British. Another indication was provided by reports from Free French agents in Brest that heavy moorings were being laid in readiness to receive a large ship (there is some doubt as to whether these reached London in time to be effective). Also, the absence of any trace of *Bismarck* anywhere near Iceland seemed puzzling. Finally, other radio messages were intercepted, which were assumed to come from *Bismarck* (in fact some of these originated from a U-boat), and were plotted between *Bismarck*'s last known position and Brittany. This time there was no mistake. It was now clear that about seven hours had been lost by steaming in the wrong direction. Tovey swung his force first to the east then to south-east on a course roughly parallel to, but far behind, the enemy. However, he had serious problems. He still did not know exactly where *Bismarck* was, but he suspected (correctly) that he had no chance of catching-up before ground-based aircraft from France would make further pursuit impossibly dangerous. After days of steaming at high speed, *King George V* was critically short of fuel. The fuel situation of his destroyers was even more serious. One by one they had to depart to replenish their bunkers, leaving Tovey's forces dangerously unprotected in an area known to be infested by U-boats. *Victorious* and her escorts had conformed to his orders and steamed north-west, towards the Denmark Strait, and were now too far away to play any further part in the action. In any case they also urgently needed to refuel, and made for Iceland to do so. Another serious potential danger was a sortie by *Scharnhorst* and *Gneisenau*. No one knew for certain how badly they had been damaged by the RAF or what the condition of *Scharnhorst*'s boilers really was. If they were to put to sea and join *Bismarck* during the final stages of her run towards France, possibly accompanied by destroyers, the Germans would have a squadron strong enough to be a real threat to Tovey's battleships and to Force H.

Once the correct assumption as regards the German's plans had been made, the Admiralty rapidly took further action. Force H was ordered to send out reconnaissance patrols to the north using aircraft fitted with long-range fuel tanks. A patrol of six submarines was ordered 120 miles off the Brittany coast as a last-ditch trap for *Bismarck*. (In fact bad weather would probably have made them as ineffective as German submarines proved to be during this particular operation.) A force consisting of four powerful Tribal Class destroyers and a Polish destroyer, under Captain Vian, was detached from escorting a troop convoy and placed under Tovey's command to act as an anti-submarine screen.

RAF Coastal Command had concluded at an early stage that the enemy destination would be Brest or St Nazaire, and acted on this assumption before their naval colleagues. The officer commanding Coastal Command, Air Marshal Sir Frederick Bowhill, was himself an ex-merchant navy officer, and had also served in the Royal Navy before transferring to the RAF. He was no stranger to air-sea operations, having participated as captain of the seaplane carrier *Empress* in the first-ever sea-launched air strike – the raid on the airship sheds near Cuxhaven in 1915. Not only did he correctly guess the destination chosen by Lutjens, he also used his experience as a seaman to determine that *Bismarck* would steer slightly south of a direct line towards it, so as to keep open the option of a landfall on the Spanish coast or at La Pallice. The high cliffs of Brittany would make a convenient landfall for her navigator. At his instigation, long-range Catalina aircraft based in Northern Ireland were ordered to search the route between the enemy's last known position and the French coast, paying particular attention to an area just south of the direct line between them.

The far-sighted decision by this highly experienced officer was to prove critical to the success of the whole operation, and is an excellent example of inter-service co-operation effected by an air force commander with an intimate understanding of the sea

The twin-engined Catalina, otherwise called the 'PBY', flying-boat was indeed a remarkable aircraft. It had entered service with the US Navy in 1936 and soon proved itself to be an immensely capable machine, with an endurance of over twenty hours in the air when long-range fuel tanks were fitted. It was robust and reliable, and its high wing made it an excellent observation platform. Obviously such an aircraft would be invaluable in the Battle of the Atlantic, and as the USA began to release strategic material to the beleaguered British under the lend-lease scheme, Catalinas came high on the list of desirable aircraft. Operating aircraft like the Catalina effectively in wartime conditions was somewhat outside the experience of both the RAF and the US Navy. Flying such a long-range, slow aircraft over the ocean required very accurate navigation, as there was seldom anything to see except the sea surface, and unless the sky was clear enough to use astro-navigation, drift had to be calculated by observing the wave tops. If the aircraft was flying at 100 knots and the wind was, for example, 50 knots, any error of judgement of rate or direction of drift would be fatal. The Catalina's long endurance meant that the crew had to be able to eat and sleep aboard the aircraft in flight. Catalinas were fitted with a reliable automatic pilot, but they carried two 'real' pilots as well, and the first deliveries of them to the RAF arrived with seventeen US Navy officers, who helped familiarise the British crews with the aircraft. At the same time they frequently but unofficially flew as second pilot on operations. As well as helping the RAF, these USN personnel were intended to gain operational experience so as to be able to play a key role should the USA become involved in war with Germany or Japan. At 03.45 hrs on 26 May, two Catalinas, PBYs M and Z of 209 Squadron RAF Coastal Command, took off from Loch Erne in Northern Ireland and climbed to their cruising height of 3,000 feet. The Irish government secretly co-operated with the British in allowing aircraft based on Loch Erne to overfly their territory on the way to the west Atlantic. On board PBY-Z the pilot, Flying Officer Briggs, was at the controls, and alongside him was Ensign Smith USN, acting as second pilot. Coastal Command crews spent many hundreds of hours flying low in noisy, bumpy, smelly aircraft, often seeing nothing but cloud and water for patrol after patrol. It was extremely boring work, but any inattention by the navigator, a wrong calculation of wind strength or direction, or of compass variation, for example, could be fatal to the whole crew. Also, failure to keep a good lookout for small objects such as a U-boat would render the whole tedious mission useless. Once out over the Atlantic, the two

PBYs dropped down to 500 feet, below the cloud base, and were buffeted and shaken by the turbulence caused by the 30–40 kt north-westerly wind. It blew directly against them, reducing speed over the surface to 80–90 knots. In places the whole face of the sea was shrouded in mist, but in the clear patches the crews could see five or six miles. At about 09.45, after six uncomfortable hours of flying, they reached their assigned area and commenced a pre-arranged search pattern. RAF Coastal Command, as we have seen, had correctly guessed that the quarry might have shaped a course a little south of the direct line to Brest and St Nazaire, and had ordered the search on this assumption. Coastal Command's foresight on this occasion was to save the day for the British.

In the rear of the aircraft, crewmen were cooking bacon and eggs, and the pilots took turns to go aft and relax over breakfast. The American, Smith, was at the controls of PBY-Z when at 10.10 he sighted a faint dark shape at the limit of visibility. Yelling for Briggs, he steered towards the object. It was certainly a large warship, and was steaming fast towards them on a south-easterly course. It was too far away to identify, but unlike British ships, it had no escorting destroyers: surely it must be German. Briggs scrambled back to the radio room while Smith opened the throttles and climbed up through the cloud, hoping to break through it and descend directly over the target to take a better look. As he dived over his target the *Bismarck*'s alert gunners greeted the plane with a barrage of fire. Holes appeared all over the wings and fuselage, and a single shell pierced the hull directly between the two pilots' seats. The aircraft was thrown violently about by exploding heavy AA shells. There was no lethal damage, however, and PBY-Z was soon joined by PBY-M in the area of the target. The position reported by Briggs's radio message was about twenty miles out, and after a few minutes the ship disappeared into the murk, but the damage had been done. The British now knew roughly where *Bismarck* was, her course and her speed. An hour later she was spotted by a Swordfish sweeping north from Sommerville's Force H, and for the rest of the day she remained under observation by other Catalinas and by *Ark Royal*'s reconnaissance patrols. With a job well done, PBY-Z made it safely back to Loch Erne. Briggs, who survived the war and took up a career in civil aviation, was ever afterwards known as 'Briggs of the *Bismarck*'.

Aboard *Bismarck* the morale boost resulting from the failure of *Victorious*'s air strike had soon began to wane. This was accelerated by no less a person than Lutjens himself, who in another atypical and ill-judged fit of loquaciousness made an address over the loudspeakers to the whole crew:

> Seamen of the Bismarck, you have covered yourselves with glory. The sinking of the Hood has not only military but also psychological value, for she was the pride of England. Henceforth the enemy will try to concentrate his forces and bring them into action against us. I therefore released Prinz Eugen at noon yesterday so that she could conduct commerce warfare on her own. She has managed to evade the enemy. We on the other hand, because of the hits we have received have been ordered [*sic*] to proceed to a French port. On our way there the enemy will gather and give us battle. The German people are with you and we will fight until our gun barrels glow red hot and the last shell has left the barrels. For us seamen the question now is victory or death.

The effect of this was devastating, suggesting as it did that an overpowering British force stood between them and their objective. The ship's officers noticed the dejected attitude of the crew, and Captain Lindemann realised that he had to do something. He made an address himself to the crew, saying clearly that the British had been out-fought and outwitted, and soon they would be in range of aircraft from France and all would be well. The crew liked and trusted their captain, and his words were a great comfort to them. Informed opinion among the ship's officers was uncertain. They had a fair idea from radio intercepts where the British were. If they could keep up a speed of 22 knots and if fuel supplies held out, they might just keep far enough ahead of Tovey's battleships to make it. They were not too worried about British submarines: it is extremely

1. HMS *Norfolk* She was one of the early County Class 8″ heavy cruisers built by Fairfields and launched in 1928. Refitted in 1939, she was damaged by a torpedo from U-47 which exploded near her, and also by an air raid. She was fitted with Type 286 radar in October 1940. She was the flagship of Rear Admiral Wake-Walker patrolling the Denmark Straight and came under fire from *Bismarck's* 15″ main armament several times, but suffered no serious damage. She played a critical part in the final battle of the *Bismarck* episode. Wake-Walker and *Norfolk's* Captain Phillips showed commendable aggression throughout the action. (*IWM FL1864*)

2. HMS *King George V* was virtually identical to *Prince of Wales*. She served as Tovey's flagship throughout the action. She was the first of five battleships of her class, being commissioned in 1940. She was fitted with 14" guns, in conformity with the maximums allowed under the ineffective Second London Naval Treaty. Originally the design had called for twelve gun main armament but this was reduced to ten in the interests of stability and armour protection. Unfortunately the British 14" turret proved unreliable in service. This was evident in the final fight with *Bismarck* when both A and Y turrets suffered serious problems. Although she was heavily armoured over most of her hull, the loss of *Prince of Wales* in 1942 showed that protection was inadequate in the face of Japanese air launched torpedoes. Her 28-knot maximum speed was inferior to most of her contemporaries and her endurance was also limited. (IWM FL14410)

3. HMS *Hood* was a stately and potent looking ship, *very fast and heavily armed. However she was derived from the battle cruisers which had proved so wanting during the battle of Jutland, and shared their inadequate armour and fire director system. She should never have been committed to combat against a powerful battleship like *Bismarck*. A particular weakness was her deck armour which made her very vulnerable to long range plunging shells. (IWM FL74)

4. HMS *Sheffield* was attached to Force H. She was a 6″ light cruiser built by Vickers and commissioned in 1937. Most unusually many of her fittings were of stainless steel instead of brass, hence the nickname 'Shiny Sheff'. It is difficult to understand how Swordfish crews mistook her slim two funnelled profile for the hump backed *Bismarck*. Her Type 79Y radar was one of the earliest shipboard installations and was used mainly for aircraft control and early warning. She kept track of *Bismarck* by radar until her set was damaged and three seamen killed when she got too close to the formidable 15″ guns. *Sheffield* went on to have a very active war, taking part in the Battle of the Barents Sea and the Battle of the North Cape. Captain Larcom had command of her

5. HMS *Rodney* and *Nelson* were the only 16″ armed battleships ever built for the Royal Navy. They were planned shortly after the First World War but the design was then drastically changed to conform to the Washington Naval Treaty. A special clause in the treaty allowed them to be built with 16″ guns as they were already planned before the treaty was concluded, but the displacement limits still applied. This resulted in most extraordinary looking ships which were slow, clumsy and had very restricted arcs of fire. She could not use her main armament on any target aft of the beam. Her main engines had to be drastically reduced to save weight, but few compromises were made in the field of armour protection so she would have been a tough opponent for any adversary which she managed to catch. An opportunity to show her mettle nearly occurred in March 1941 when she encountered *Scharnhorst* and *Gneisenau*, but they retired rapidly when they realised that they were up against superior fire power. After the *Bismarck* encounter she completed her voyage to the US for engine repairs, then was allocated to Force H at Gibraltar with whom she had an active part in numerous convoy and invasion support operations. In 1944 her massive fire power was deployed to good effect against German fortifications in Normandy. She ended her service supporting Murmansk convoys. *(IWM FL9690)*

6. A Swordfish approaching low over a relatively calm sea. The very low wing loading of these aircraft made them able to operate and manoeuvre very close to the surface of the sea, so they were difficult for defenders to hit with gunfire. The three crewmen must have become extremely cold and uncomfortable during long range operations, nevertheless the 'Stringbag' was very popular with pilots and proved itself able to carry out successful attacks against heavily defended targets. Its Bristol Pegasus engine was a by word for reliability. (*IWM A4100*)

7. Admiral Somerville and Captain Maund in tropical gear. The photograph illustrates the excellent spirit of co-operation between the admiral and a captain under his command. Somerville was an outstanding leader who was able to get the very best out of the crews of his ships and aircraft. Maund was of a similar type, and very popular with the Fleet Air Arm contingent on *Ark Royal*. Somerville went on to command British naval forces in the Pacific in the last stages of the war. Maund was court marshalled after the sinking of *Ark Royal* by a U-boat in November 1941, near Gibraltar. Although all but one of *Ark*'s crew were saved, Maund was found not to have taken sufficiently effective measures to prevent the loss of the ship. His naval career was not seriously compromised by this and he reached the rank of Rear Admiral. (*IWM A5825*)

8. *Bismarck* in trouble. This picture taken from *Prinz Eugen* early on 24 May shows her labouring under the effects of the water flooding into the forward compartments due to hits from *Prince of Wales*. *Prinz* was dropping astern to see if there was evidence of oil leaking out of *Bismarck's* tanks. The bow down trim was never fully corrected and must have made her burn more fuel than usual. Suggestions that it could be corrected by jettisoning the anchors and chain were rejected. (*IWM HN400*)

9. Aircraft on board *Victorious*. This gives an impression of how difficult and dangerous it was to work aircraft on deck in a rough sea and strong head wind. Wings had to be unfolded and engines started on deck and somehow the aircraft themselves had to be prevented from breaking loose. *Victorious* was newly commissioned at the time of the *Bismarck* episode. Unlike earlier aircraft carriers she had an armoured deck. (*IWM A4090*)

10. A Catalina flying boat. Catalinas had an endurance, when fitted with long range tanks, of 24 hours or more. They had a moderately comfortable ward room and bunks for off duty crew, although this area got very cramped when long range tanks were carried, and smelt horribly of petrol. There was excellent visibility from the nose and the blister turrets amidships. These tough, reliable, aircraft were instrumental in achieving the defeat of the U-boat menace in the Atlantic, and the destruction of the Japanese lines of communication in the Pacific. Good co-operation between RAF Coastal Command, which operated them, and the Royal Navy was vital to the success of naval operations in the Atlantic. The RAF took delivery of 650 of over 3,000 Catalinas produced during the war. Most Catilinas were flying boats only, a few had wheels enabling them to serve as amphibians. (*IWM CH2455*)

difficult for a submarine to manoeuvre so as to intercept a fast-moving warship, and indeed, as they were to find out themselves, interception is impossible in heavy weather when the submarine's surface speed has to be reduced. The main worry was aircraft. They knew that Force H with its carrier was somewhere to the south-west of them and might be able to launch an attack, but it was also clear by now that the enemy did not know exactly where they were, and with luck the strike aircraft would not find them. To make things more confusing for any British forces they might encounter, the engineering staff were instructed to build a dummy funnel, which might lead attacking aircraft or ships to mistake *Bismarck* at long range for a British heavy cruiser. In fact the dummy was never erected, but building it probably raised morale on board. There was plenty of other work for the engineering staff to do. The damage to the port boiler room and the flooding there caused by *Prince of Wales*'s hit was threatening to allow salt water to get into the main engines and cause serious damage. This was corrected by draining the salt water out of the system and bringing more condenser capacity on stream to supply fresh water to the main engines. An even more difficult task was to try to recover some of the fuel oil in the damaged forward compartments. Much of this had by now leaked out, but eventually men in diving-gear managed to get to the valves and release some of the remaining precious liquid into the main tanks. There was a suggestion that they should jettison the main anchors and chain to correct the bow-down attitude of the ship caused by the flooding of the forward compartments. This would have enabled her to go faster or burn less fuel. It was rejected as being too risky.

On shore the naval HQ in Paris was keeping busy anticipating the arrival of the great ship. A signal was sent to tell Lutjens that port facilities in Brest, St Nazaire and La Pallice were ready to receive him. A U-boat deployment along his route was said to be in place (actually it wasn't), and long-range Condor aircraft, fighters and bombers were readied (at least in theory) to give cover. Three destroyers were detailed to meet *Bismarck* off the coast. Luckily for the British, many of these measures were frustrated by the rising gale. The destroyers could not put to sea. Aircraft were unable to take off in the high winds and poor visibility, and the U-boats could not make headway on the surface. Only one, *U.556*, returning from a successful Atlantic patrol, was able to get near, and she had no remaining torpedoes and was critically low on fuel, and so, as we shall see, she was nothing more than a passive spectator of the action to come. An announcement was made, however, in the early morning of 26 May to stimulate the crew, and especially the engineers, in their efforts:

> We have now passed three-quarters of Ireland on our way to St Nazaire. Around noon we will be in the U-boats' operational area and within range of German aircraft. We can count on the appearance of Condor planes after 12.00.

Morale on board soared. They were going to make it!

But next morning everything changed. The appearance of PBY-Z, whose radio transmission was picked up by the *B-Dienst* team on board, made it clear that the cloak of invisibility that had sheltered *Bismarck* was penetrated. Lindemann thought about sending up one of his Arado float-planes to shoot down the Catalina, but it was considered too dangerous to allow the aircraft to operate in such stormy weather. This seems an odd decision, as does the inactivity of the Arados during the rest of the action. It is true that the sea was too rough for the float-planes to land and be recovered intact. However, British planes operated successfully in the prevailing conditions, and it was quite common practice to launch fighters from ships in conditions in which they could not be recovered, allowing them to ditch in the sea and rescuing the crew from the water. An alternative would have been for the aircraft to fly eastwards with the following wind towards the coast after being in action. It would have been close to the shore by the time it ran out of fuel, and could have been recovered by coastal forces. The Arado was a formidable fighter, and had it found the PBY there could only have been one outcome. The Germans had no way of knowing that PBY-Z's message had been picked up by anyone except themselves, and it would surely have been worth losing a plane or two to keep their position hidden from the enemy.

Even more unwelcome events for the Germans were to follow. The sight of the Swordfish an hour later made it obvious that there was a carrier in the locality, and there was going to be an attack in due course. Even this threat did not induce Lutjens to use the available aircraft. Just one of them aloft could have made attacks by slow-moving torpedo-bombers much more difficult. One gets the impression that Lindemann had little confidence in his *Luftwaffe* team.

Bismarck's course for the rest of the day was to be dogged by aircraft staying just out of range, a sinister reminder of what might be to come.

On board *King George V* Tovey was now able to make a proper assessment of the situation. *Bismarck* was now 700 miles from St Nazaire, only about thirty-six hours' steaming. By dawn the following morning, 27 May, she would be in range of shore-based bombers and long-range fighters, and the hunt by British surface-ships and aircraft would become extremely hazardous. In any case, by that time *King George V* would not have enough fuel to fight and then get home. She was some 150 miles – six hours' steaming – behind *Bismarck* on a parallel course. *Rodney* was closer, only 125 miles away, thanks to the deliberate refusal of her captain to conform to orders, but she was too slow to have a hope of catching up. *King George V* could not possibly get close enough to open fire on *Bismarck* before she was safely under friendly air cover.

Force H, however, was just over a hundred miles from the enemy, east-south-east and in a position to intercept her course. But Force H had only one heavy ship, the old battle cruiser *Renown* – smaller, more lightly armed and even less protected than *Hood*. Somerville had suggested that if he got upwind of the enemy and made use of smoke to cover himself he might be able to use *Renown*'s 15-inch guns to do enough damage to slow the enemy down and allow *King George V* and *Rodney* to catch up. Everyone knew that the scheme was a desperate one and would almost certainly result in the loss of *Renown*, and this plan was eventually vetoed. The British submarines were trying to get into position to intercept, but they represented only a faint hope. The only realistic possibility was to use *Ark Royal*'s aircraft to strike *Bismarck* before she came under the umbrella of shore-based *Luftwaffe* aircraft. That meant she had to be hit before nightfall. Tovey was desperately tired. He had had to contend with all the problems of marshalling the forces under him, with the now rapidly deteriorating weather, with the serious fuel state of his ships and with the terrible responsibility he felt for the lives of the men he commanded. On top of all this he was still being deluged with orders and suggestions from London. Why had the cruisers not attacked with torpedoes? Don't worry about *King George V*'s fuel state, she could be towed home after the battle (an absurd suggestion, which could only have come from Churchill). The Admiralty complained that it could not visualise the situation clearly, and called for further information so that it could give the requisite orders. (What orders? Surely Tovey was the commander at sea, shouldn't he be giving any necessary orders?) Through all this Tovey kept his head. He ordered Somerville to use the light cruiser *Sheffield* to shadow *Bismarck* and to ready *Ark Royal*'s aircraft for a strike. *Sheffield* was lightly armed and had almost no protective armour, but she was a fast ship and could close *Bismarck* rapidly, even though it meant steaming at high speed into the teeth of a rising gale. She was also well accustomed to working with *Ark Royal*'s aircraft, using her radar to assist in locating the target. She was the ideal ship to act as a marker for attacking squadrons. Captain Vian, leading the destroyers towards their rendezvous with Tovey, also picked up the signal that *Bismarck* had been found. Making up his mind to ignore orders and use his own initiative, he turned his ships round and steamed at full speed to intercept. The sea was by now so rough that the destroyers were almost impossible to handle before the following wind. They were in constant danger of broaching or even capsizing. One seaman was washed overboard and lost, and several were injured. Speed had to be drastically reduced.

Ark Royal seems to have been an especially happy ship. She was a large carrier of 28,000 tons with a complement of up to sixty aircraft and a top speed of 31 knots. She was in fact the first British ship to be designed from scratch as an aircraft carrier. Earlier carriers had been conversions of half-built cruisers or battle cruisers. Her design had been compromised by treaty limitations and she did not have an armoured deck, unlike later

British fleet carriers. By May 1941 she had steamed over 100,000 miles since her last refit, and was experiencing some problems with her propulsion gear, but these did not compromise her operational efficiency. Her captain, Maund, was a popular and excellent leader, and worked well with Somerville, his chief. Somerville himself had gained enormous respect by risking his ships to pick up ditched airmen in the Mediterranean. The aircrews also liked the ship because she had excellent accommodation and a can-do attitude among the crew that made life more tolerable for everyone. For example, they never returned from flying duties without the possibility of a good hot meal. This was in stark contrast to some carriers, where the seamen regarded flyers as nothing better than a nuisance. Aircrews were kept busy with plenty of flying, and they knew that the whole team on the ship was behind them. One of the peculiarities of serving on the *Ark* was that flyers, including senior pilots, were required to operate the ship's defensive armament when they were not flying. That meant that aircrews not detailed to fly would be trying to shoot down attacking enemy aircraft. They got plenty of experience of doing this for real in the Mediterranean, and this work enabled them to learn at first hand exactly how an attacking pilot could make things difficult for defenders. We shall see how this was to prove invaluable in their subsequent operations. They were keen to have a crack at *Bismarck*, having been disappointed in March when they came within an ace of getting in a strike on *Scharnhorst* and *Gneisenau* at the end of their Atlantic foray. They also firmly believed, and with some justification, that they were the most experienced naval air group in existence. They had been following developments in the chase after *Bismarck* closely, but had not been informed that she had separated from *Prinz Eugen* or that she had suffered damage and a fuel leak. In fact no one in Force H knew this for certain, nor did they know what *Prinz Eugen*, *Scharnhorst* and *Gneisenau* were doing. On the morning of the 26th the *Ark* was battling with a north-westerly gale, which sent wisps of spray up as high as the bridge. She had had to reduce speed from 27 knots to 17 during the night as a result of the heavy seas, but still she was pitching wildly. At times the fore part of the flight deck would dig into an oncoming wave, drenching everything on deck with spray. The navigating officer was sent forward to measure the movement on the flight deck, and recorded a fifty-six-foot rise and fall. As soon as the order to search for *Bismarck* was received however, ten Swordfish were brought up on deck and extra gangs of seamen were ordered to help to hold them from being blown off the deck. Combined with the forward speed of the ship, the wind over the deck was about 50 knots – almost enough to allow the aircraft to take off without moving forward. They formed up and carried out a search, each aircraft covering an assigned rectangular area to the west and north-west of the carrier. Each aircraft would be up for about three-and-a-half hours, their crews buffeted by the slipstream in their open cockpits, deafened by the roar of the engines. While the machines were in the air, the *Ark*'s radio room had intercepted the transmission from Briggs's Catalina, reporting his sighting. Twenty minutes after receiving this report, about an hour after Briggs's sighting, Sub-Lieutenant Elias, flying one of the Swordfish, saw a large ship beneath him. He was not certain of her identity – no one knew at this stage that *Prinz Eugen* and *Bismarck* had separated, and there were rumours that *Scharnhorst* was also at sea. All the German ships looked similar from a distance, with a single funnel and a huge, ugly hump amidships. He reported his sighting immediately, and was soon joined by another Swordfish, which confirmed his observation and position.

The pace of activity on *Ark Royal* became furious. The original search team was now due to return, and six more aircraft fitted with long-range tanks had to be prepared to maintain visual contact. At the same time an attack force of Swordfish carrying duplex-fused torpedoes was being prepared. Duplex fuses were designed to enable the torpedoes – 'kippers', as they were called by the crews – to run deep under the target so that they could explode where they would do most damage. They were triggered magnetically or by impact.

The returning search patrol now had the problem of landing on the violently heaving deck of the carrier. Conditions were now described officially as 'extremely severe and entailing great hazard to aircraft'. If a descending aircraft hit the rising deck of the carrier it would be bounced like a ping-pong ball into the air and flung into the water. One aircraft had a narrow escape, its undercarriage and lower wing being crushed by the impact, but the crew were unhurt, and the wreckage was eventually cleared away, allowing the others to land safely. The delay had meant that the remaining aircraft were down to their last few drops of fuel. Elias and other members of the crews who had made the sighting were immediately summoned to the bridge and closely questioned to try to ascertain which ship they had seen. Eventually Captain Maund was satisfied and informed Somerville on *Renown* that the ship seen was definitely *Bismarck*.

Positioning a carrier to launch a strike with slow-moving aircraft in a strong wind is no easy matter. The ship must be as close to the enemy as possible, but not so close as to risk coming under fire. She then has to steam into wind while the aircraft are launched, and again while they are recovered. At these points she is extremely vulnerable. In the prevailing circumstances *Bismarck* was steaming directly downwind, and so would be on the opposite course to *Ark Royal* as she launched, closing her at some 40 knots. Somerville chose to take up a position on the north-eastern flank of *Bismarck*. Captain Maund, a consummate seaman, quickly manoeuvred into the launch position in spite of the heavy seas. *Sheffield* had already been ordered to close *Bismarck* at high speed and act as a beacon for the attacking aircraft.

By the time the strike force of fifteen machines was ready to take off, at 14.45 hrs, about four hours after the first sighting, *Sheffield* was well on her way towards the target. The attack crews of 820 and 810 Squadrons Fleet Air Arm were all experienced flyers and had been fully briefed on their mission. The lead aircraft of each section had air-to-surface radar, extremely useful for finding a target in the poor visibility prevailing. As well as the Swordfish, *Ark Royal*, like *Victorious*, carried a complement of Fairy Fulmar fighters. *Ark Royal* had readied her Fulmars for operation, but the weather conditions were such that it was eventually decided to leave them behind. Only the frail-looking Swordfish could tackle operating from a pitching carrier in an Atlantic gale that battered ships and grounded the *Luftwaffe*.

A minute after take-off, one of the fifteen was forced to return due to engine trouble, unusual for the normally trusty Bristol Pegasus that powered the Swordfish. The pilot had to turn and land back on the carrier with a full load of fuel and a torpedo, an extremely dangerous operation, which was completed without incident. The other fourteen flew on through thick cloud. *Bismarck* was supposed to be 50–60 miles to the west of them. A little earlier than expected, the lead aircraft picked up a radar echo – a large ship steaming fast westwards. The aircraft could not talk to each other by radio, as they only had direct radio contact with *Ark Royal*, so communication between Swordfish was by hand signal. The leading aircraft alerted the rest and signalled them to commence their attack. The Swordfish dropped down below the cloud base and saw their target. She was steaming at high speed, with fumes pouring out of her two funnels. The aircraft split up so as to attack from different, pre-selected bearings, thus confusing the gunners and making it difficult for the ship to comb torpedo tracks. Luckily, it seemed, they had not yet been spotted, as there was no flak, and the first two sections of aircraft started their torpedo-firing run. The lead machine, piloted by Sub-Lieutenant Mike Lithgow (later to become famous as a test pilot on supersonic jets) dived in to the attack. As the torpedoes were released, the ship eventually seemed to sense danger, and she increased to emergency maximum speed, seeming almost to leap out of the water, and turned towards the attack so as to comb the torpedo tracks. There were two explosions some distance from the target. The unreliable duplex heads had detonated on hitting the water. The other weapons seemed to run true, but passed harmlessly beneath the ship, three of them exploding in the water well beyond her. The three last machines lined up to make a final attack when their leader, Lieutenant Commander Stewart-More, sensed something wrong. Somehow the target looked familiar. A signal light flashed from its bridge. It was *Sheffield*'s recognition code! Horrified, he pulled out of his dive, signalling urgently to the two aircraft in his section. Pull out! Pull out! How could the others possibly have made such a stupid mistake. Here was a ship with two funnels – the German ships all had only one. There had been no return fire, although *Sheffield*'s crew must have been sorely tempted. In any case *Sheffield* was a ship they had known and worked with for months. There could be no excuses. Mortified, they flew back to *Ark Royal* to face the music. The gunner in the lead aircraft at least retained his sense of humour. He signalled to the offended *Sheffield*, 'Sorry for kipper.'

All fourteen made it safely back to *Ark Royal*, but there was one further incident. Three Swordfish were still carrying their torpedoes, as they had not fired at *Sheffield*. They were ordered to jettison their weapons so as to reduce weight for landing. One failed to release and the aircraft landed heavily with it in place. The jolt freed the torpedo, which then rolled from side to side across the lurching deck, a shower of sparks coming from it. Eventually it was captured by a party of seamen and disposed of. The dejected crews were debriefed. Captain Maund charitably did not inform Tovey about the attack on the wrong ship, and simply signalled, 'No hits on *Bismarck*.' As one of the observers ruefully put it, 'It was a perfect attack, right height, right range, right cloud cover, right speed and the wrong f.....g ship.' Morale on board plunged. This was a critical moment and they had miserably failed, the light was going and there was hardly time for another attack. They had let themselves and the whole fleet down. In fairness it is important to understand that the débâcle was not entirely the pilots' fault. *Ark Royal* had been told of *Sheffield*'s deployment, but somehow this news had not been passed on to the flight crews, as the signals office had been overloaded with messages. There was at that time no IFF (identification friend or foe) system by which radar could tell enemy ships from friendly ones, and visual recognition from the freezing cockpit of a plane in thick weather is not easy. Split-second decisions in such circumstances can easily be wrong.

Aboard *Bismarck*, the day had been full of foreboding. Early in the morning a lookout had spotted masts far off at the limit of visibility; these were Vian's destroyers on the way to join Tovey, and they soon disappeared. After the appearance of Briggs's Catalina, enemy aircraft were never far away. Occasionally a burst of flak would be required to drive off any that got too close. The crew knew nothing of *Sheffield*'s brush with friendly aircraft during the afternoon, for it had been just out of earshot, about twenty miles away from them. The officers knew from the presence of wheeled aircraft that a carrier must be close and that it was only a matter of time before an attack took place. Some took to wearing life-vests. But there was still hope. As evening wore on it seemed possible that there would be no attack that day, in which case, so the optimists said, they would be safely under the umbrella of the *Luftwaffe* by morning. At a little after 18.00 hrs they became aware of *Sheffield*'s presence – another ominous portent. But still nothing happened. Lutjens signalled Paris, stating that his fuel situation was serious. It is impossible to know now how much fuel *Bismarck* really had on board. Certainly she had been using it prodigally during the early part of her voyage, and while she made the futile high-speed dash down the Denmark Strait, trying to evade the shadowing cruisers. By now Lutjens must have been bitterly regretting his irresponsible decisions to put to sea without full tanks and to omit to replenish them either in the Norwegian fjord or from the tanker in the Arctic Sea. The lower speed of between 20 and 23 knots maintained during the latter part of the voyage would have conserved supplies, however, and the surviving officers later stated that they believed that she had just enough to reach France. None of these was in a position to know for certain. Morale on the lower deck throughout the day was maintained. It became known that the pursuing battleships were at least a hundred miles astern and could not catch up, and even if aircraft did attack they reasoned that they had beaten off one torpedo attack without serious damage and had destroyed, or so they were told, five aircraft. Surely they could survive another? The ship's engines continued their reassuring hum as she rode the following seas. Even the wind, which was almost directly astern, was cancelled out by the ship's forward move-ment so conditions at their action stations were tolerable. The crewmen were tired, however. They had been on alert almost continuously for three whole days and had been in action against Holland's force and against the aircraft from *Victorious*. They longed for the comfort and safety of a French port. Little did they know of the horrific ordeal which awaited them that night.

The British situation was now desperate. Unless the enemy could be slowed down and caught, Tovey would have to give up the pursuit. Neither *King George V* nor *Rodney* had enough fuel to maintain the chase beyond about 09.00 on the 27th, and he had reached the miserable conclusion that he would have to abandon the chase early the next morning, having failed to catch up. But aboard *Ark Royal* the shameful failure that afternoon had bred a new determination among the Swordfish crews. Although nightfall was approaching, they were determined to have another go at the task they had so miserably failed to achieve that afternoon, and there was no shortage of pressure from above for them to do so. This was absolutely the last realistic chance to stop *Bismarck* from escaping. There were normally more crews than serviceable aircraft on the carrier, and this time most of the crews who had taken part in the previous operation were stood down and 818 Squadron, led by Lieutenant Commander Tim Coode, was selected to carry out the attack. Already *Sheffield* had located *Bismarck*, picking her up on radar at 17.45 and making a visual sighting soon afterwards. She was the first British ship to see her for two days. *Bismarck* had, of course, been under observation by aircraft, although this had been sporadic, partly because of weather conditions and partly because the Swordfish and Catalinas often mistook each other for enemy aircraft and had chosen to take avoiding action. Now that *Sheffield* was in contact with *Bismarck*, she would be a useful staging-post for the strike aircraft as they sought for their target. Coode had insisted that the fuses on the torpedoes should be changed from the obviously unreliable duplex model to conventional impact pistols. This was against Admiralty standing instructions, but it was obvious from the attack on *Sheffield* that the duplex units were useless in the prevailing rough conditions. This meant the torpedoes would have to strike the side of the ship directly in order to explode. Depth of running was another issue. The deeper a torpedo is when it hits its target, the more damage it does, because the water pressure causes more of the energy of the explosion to be exerted onto the target, and because seawater rushes in more violently if the hole made is deep down in the target's hull. Normally a torpedo would be set at 22 feet to do maximum damage to a big ship like *Bismarck*, which drew almost 30 feet, but on *Ark Royal* many people had the impression that their torpedoes were running too deep. Also, the big sea that was running might lift the ship clean over a torpedo set at normal depth. Eventually it was agreed to set the depth at only 10 feet.

Once again the lifts brought fifteen Swordfish, rearmed and refuelled, onto the slippery deck, over which the wind was howling with renewed fury. Mechanics wound on the inertia starter handles, and fifteen Pegasus engines – 'faithful Peggy', they were called – burst into life. First a little cloud of blue smoke would issue from the exhausts and the machine would tremble as the engine ran unevenly, and then it would settle down into its deep, reassuring roar. The aircrews noticed that the sailors on deck, struggling to hold the aircraft on the plunging, slippery surface, were not their usual cheery selves, They looked grim and determined, knowing that this was the last chance for their ship to prove her worth. *Ark Royal* turned into wind and reduced speed to 12 knots for take-off, giving an apparent wind speed of 40–50 knots over the deck. As she turned she lurched and rolled, making the job of the men on deck extremely dangerous: if an aircraft broke loose or a man got too close to a propeller the consequences would be horrible. Conditions on deck were so bad that the 'batsman' – an experienced flyer who gave pilots the signals to take off and land – had to be lashed to the deck to avoid being blown overboard, but Commander Pat Stringer did his job superbly. Each aircraft was signalled to start its run when the bows were in a trough and it seemed that the plane would run away downhill and plunge into the sea, but as she moved forward the deck came up under her and away she would soar into the turbulent air. All fifteen got off safely and formed up in line astern over *Renown*. In the air it was extremely bumpy, the aircraft being thrown violently about by turbulence. *Bismarck* was only thirty-eight miles away to the south-east, with *Sheffield* shadowing her as close as she dared go – about twelve miles away, and well within range of her radar. The air over *Sheffield* was reasonably clear, but a mass of cloud had formed over *Bismarck*. In addition to the cruiser, relays of reconnaissance Swordfish were

102

still keeping watch on the great battleship. The attacking air-craft kept low as they made the short hop to *Sheffield*, and as they came overhead a signal lamp from the bridge gave them a range and bearing to their target. It had been planned that the attack should be made by five sub-flights, all approaching from different pre-arranged angles so as to divide the fire of the defenders, and make it difficult for *Bismarck* to dodge the torpedoes. The idea was to climb above the clouds and form up in their separate sub-flights so as to make a co-ordinated attack, but 'no plan survived contact with the enemy'. As they climbed up to 6,000 feet into clear air, the pilots noticed ice forming on the surfaces of the wings and on the struts. At the same time it became almost unendurably cold in the open cockpits. Icing is extremely dangerous to an aircraft as it can destroy the shape of the lifting surfaces of the wings and add weight very quickly. Before they had time to deploy as they had planned, the aircraft had to get out of the freezing air and begin their dive willy-nilly into the attack, many of them losing contact with their flight leaders as they did so in the thick blanket of cloud beneath them. At about 300 feet they suddenly burst out of the cloud into the twilight. *Bismarck*'s gunners had seen the aircraft a few seconds earlier and had a hot reception ready, once again using every weapon, including the 15-inch main armament. By this time the aircraft were completely out of their proper formation. Some spotted their target immediately and went into the attack, some faltered and some saw nothing as they burst out of the cloud cover. The accounts of what actually happened next were confused at the time and have become more so since. Several aircraft certainly lost contact with the target altogether and returned to *Sheffield* for another bearing. Two of these aircraft found the target on the second attempt and fired their torpedoes, clearly achieving one, or possibly two, hits amidships on the port side. These shook the ship violently, but exploding as they did against the torpedo bulkhead, they did only minor damage. Four other aircraft joined up to form an *ad hoc* sub-flight and attacked from the starboard side. They came under very heavy fire, one was severely damaged and its pilot, Sub-Lieutenant Swanton, and his air gunner were wounded. One of their torpedoes may possibly also have made a hit amidships. The most important blow was struck by one of two aircraft that attacked from aft on the port side. Pulling out of their dive and shutting the throttle so as to reduce speed to the prescribed 90 knots, they faced a wall of fire that buffeted their machines and hurled them off course, but the shells were all bursting well ahead of them. Probably the Germans were unable to believe how slow the approach was. Remembering his experience as a gunner on *Ark Royal*, the pilot of the leading aircraft knew that if he kept below the horizon the defenders would find him very hard to aim at as he approached, so he came down as low as he could, almost touching the wave tops. He was certainly less than fifty feet above the water. As the plane approached to about 500 yards from the target, the observer watched the waves underneath the plane. It was no good releasing onto the crest of a wave, which would knock the weapon off course. 'Now!' he yelled, and the torpedo streaked away, running true towards the target. As it did so it seemed that the ship turned to starboard, thrusting its stern towards the incoming missile. Directly behind this aircraft – the pilot was Sub-Lieutenant Moffat – was another Swordfish, flown by Lieutenant Keane. He followed the same procedure as Moffat, loosing his weapon a few seconds later. His observer thought he saw a massive explosion towards the stern of the ship, but he could not say whose torpedo was responsible.

A strange incident took place soon after the attacking planes had taken off from *Ark Royal*. *U.556*, which had been return-ing from patrol, was monitoring radio traffic from *Bismarck*, and tried to get close to her in case she could assist. She had had a successful patrol but was now very low on fuel and had expended her last torpedo finishing-off a damaged freighter. As she was running before the following seas, a lookout spotted two large warships coming towards them. *U.556* dived quickly and levelled off at periscope depth. Her captain, Herbert Wohlfarth, a highly experienced commander, peered into his periscope and could hardly believe his eyes. Coming right towards him, only a few hundred yards away, were *Ark Royal* and *Renown*. He could see the next relay of reconnaissance Swordfish on *Ark Royal*'s deck getting ready to take off. The big ships were not zigzagging and they had no destroyer escort.

Two torpedoes could have finished them both, and at that range he could hardly have missed. But he had no torpedoes.

As the attacking Swordfish turned away, the blanket of cloud that had surrounded *Bismarck* lifted a little, and her gun directors were able to see *Sheffield* about nine miles away to the south-west, well within range. The first salvo was short, but the second straddled her, showering her with splinters, killing three men and wounding six others. *Sheffield* rapidly made off, making smoke as she did so. Apart from the casualties, she suffered one other important item of damage – her vital radar. She would now have to shadow by visual means.

Having released their weapons, Moffat and Keane had to turn and accelerate away from the ship, keeping as low as possible until they were out of danger – full throttle and full right rudder, keeping the turn flat as only a Swordfish could, to avoid presenting a silhouette to the gunners. All the aircraft got back safely and landed without incident, although several had to be written-off due to the damage suffered from flak. One had 127 holes in her made by enemy gunfire. Swanton and his gunner were found not to be badly injured, and none of the other flyers had been hurt. There was no rejoicing on board. The crews thought they had made one or two hits, but it did not seem to them that *Bismarck* had been damaged severely. The utter confusion that had reigned during the attack made it impossible to piece together a picture of what had actually happened. Certainly no one had hung around to watch for torpedo strikes or decide who had fired which weapon. The exhausted crews sat down to a hot meal, which few of them could eat, and as many machines as could be made serviceable were prepared for a third attempt, planned to be made at first light, in the knowledge that this time the *Luftwaffe* would be in a position to intervene. There were only just enough torpedoes left on board for one more strike. *Ark Royal* signalled Tovey to inform him that it did not seem that the attack had been successful. No one on *Ark Royal* claimed to have made a certain hit, and it has never been established beyond doubt which aircraft made a successful attack. This says a great deal about the team spirit that was so strong a characteristic of *Ark Royal*'s complement.

Tovey's force had by now been strengthened by the arrival of *Rodney*. She must have made an amazing sight for the crew of *King George V* as she appeared, battling through the stormy seas, her huge foredeck plunging under water as far as the three great triple 16-inch turrets. She seemed to them to have been cut off just aft of the main mast as if the builders had forgotten to finish her off. Tovey asked her what speed she could make and she replied '22 knots', so *King George V* slowed to that speed. Shortly afterwards another signal from *Rodney*: 'Your 22 knots seems a little faster than ours.' Tovey slowed down again. He said he could almost hear the old warhorse panting for breath. Strange though she appeared, *Rodney*'s powerful artillery was a welcome addition to the force, especially as *Prince of Wales* had been forced to depart to refuel.

Shortly after *Ark Royal*'s disappointing signal, *Sheffield*, which had remained in visual contact, sent a different report to Tovey, an extraordinary report: 'Enemy steering north-east.' North-east? Directly towards his pursuing battleships? Impossible! Tovey remarked sourly that *Sheffield*'s captain must have joined the 180-degree club – making the same mistake as his own staff had made the day before. But no. *Sheffield* repeated her signal and stated that the target had also slowed right down. This news was then confirmed by the last of the shadowing aircraft: 'Enemy stopped. Enemy heading north.' This machine did not land on *Ark Royal* until about midnight, but its crew's evidence was conclusive. They had seen *Bismarck* make two complete circles and then stop dead in the water. She then assumed an unsteady course, moving slowly northwards. Here was hard evidence that *Bismarck* had been severely damaged, and Tovey might yet catch her. He held a quick council of war. His ships could be upon her before dawn, and using their radar to locate her, smash her to pieces before she had a chance to repair whatever was wrong with her machinery. That was superficially attractive, and also would reduce the time *King George V* had to remain at sea, so easing the fuel situation. But Tovey rejected it. He had seen enough of the night fighting at Jutland to know what an uncertain affair it can be. Ships are incorrectly identified. Accurate gunnery is difficult, especially in rough weather when shell splashes are hard to see. 'Friendly-fire' incidents are a constant danger. A single battleship might gain an advantage over two attackers. No, he would wait until morning, but in the meantime he would use his destroyers to harry the enemy during the night. Before catching a few hours' well-earned sleep, Tovey, a devout Christian, knelt down to thank God for the events of the day and pray fervently for those who would be in action on the morrow.

CHAPTER 7

The Finale

Vian's Tribal Class destroyers were fine, modern vessels, all completed in 1938 or 1939. They were very fast, able to make 36.5 knots and had eight 4.7-inch guns, but their main armament was their four 21-inch torpedo tubes. They were accompanied by the Polish destroyer *Piorun*. As we have seen, they had had a rough ride from their convoy duty, first to join the battleships and then to close the enemy. They were now steaming at 27 knots stern on to the sea, which made them roll abominably and must have sorely tested the stomachs of the seamen. They were near the limits of their sea-keeping capability. However, Vian was a tough and determined leader, and he continued to speed towards the wounded battleship. Some of *Ark Royal's* aircraft sighted them in the failing light and remarked what a magnificent sight they made.

We must now return to *Bismarck* herself and how she fared during the fatal attack by the Swordfish. The gunners had sighted the aircraft briefly before they came in to the attack. They then disappeared into cloud, then seemed to come swarming down from all directions. Lindemann, on the bridge, was frantically shouting helm orders as he watched each plane come in towards him, but the attacks were so haphazard and unpredictable that he could do little to avoid the oncoming torpedo tracks. This time the ship used every gun she had against her attackers, the 15-inch main armament as before to raise splashes, and the 6-inch secondary armament, as fast as the guns could be fired, into the sea in an attempt to deflect the torpedoes, while the sixteen director-controlled anti-aircraft guns concentrated on hitting the aircraft as soon as they emerged from cloud. The gunners operating the light quick firers and automatics were instructed not to take too much care about their aim, just get off as many rounds as possible in the right direction. They noticed that the Swordfish seemed to hang almost stationary just above the sea, so low that their undercarriages were invisible. The pilots, they noticed, seemed totally undeterred by the gunfire. The ship felt the jar of the first torpedo strike (it was never finally determined if there was one, two or three of these) amidships, against the heavy armour of the anti-torpedo belt. Not too much to worry them there. Then something completely different. Two planes approached from the port beam and seemed to veer to the right as the ship herself was beginning to swing to starboard. Then a horrible crash from the aft part of the ship, and she seemed to buck as a shock-wave running forward down the length of the hull displaced deck plates in the engine room and caused the whole hull to ripple as it ran forward. The ship started a sharp turn to port, heeling as she did so, until it seemed she must capsize as the great Atlantic waves came from abeam. She righted herself, stopping dead in the water, engines stopped, as the crew looked around them in horror. The attack seemed to be over. It had lasted only fifteen or twenty minutes, but *Bismarck* was in a dire situation. The torpedo had struck her at her weakest point, about twenty feet under water, close to the twin rudders. (What a good decision it had been to set the running depth of the torpedoes at ten feet, as set at the officially prescribed depth the weapon would have passed clean under her). The shock had caused the safety valves on the main engine controls to cut off steam, which was why the engines had stopped dead. Water surged up the distorted port propeller shaft and partly flooded the engine-room, and worst of all the aft steering-room with the steering-gear and motors was open to the sea, with the rudders jammed twelve degrees to port. Engineers only took a few minutes to reseal the propeller shaft and pump out the engine rooms so that power was restored and the engines could be restarted, but the ship was still unmanageable. Whatever combination of propellers was used, she would not steer in any direction except roughly into wind, veering thirty degrees or so from side to side. Extra men had to be drafted into the engine-room to handle the control valves as the bridge constantly called for changes to try to keep her on course. 'Full ahead port, stop starboard. Full astern starboard, half ahead centre and port. Stop port full ahead centre.' The temperature in the engine-room was a scorching 50°C, but the struggle went on all night, men toiling and sweating at the controls.

But something must be done to gain control of the rudders, or at least neutralise them. The first idea was to blow them off with explosive. There were volunteers to go over the stern and set charges against the rudders from the outside. This was rejected as impossible in the rough sea. Blowing them off from inside risked blowing the whole stern off the ship and sinking her. Someone suggested using the door of the aircraft hangar to act as an extra rudder, offsetting the damaged ones, but it soon proved impossible to rig this device.

Restoring proper operation of the rudders themselves was the only hope, but this too seemed impossible. The steering-room in the stern of the ship had been flooded and the water-tight bulkheads forward of it had had to be shored up and the armoured hatches closed to prevent further flooding. Water in the steering-rooms, which contained the steering-motors and mechanical linkage, was sloshing to and fro with the motion of the ship. Attempts were made to pump it out, but water in the starters of the pump motors made this impossible. A team of engineers then attempted to get at the rudder heads from on deck. They found that access to them was made impossible even with diving-gear, as the ship was pitching so violently that water was surging in and out of the stern compartment and anyone entering it would immediately have been smashed to pieces. Later on, it did prove possible to fit an emergency tiller over one of the rudder yokes, but it was impossible to operate because of the oil and water swilling about in the steering-room. Attempts to place collision mats over the great hole in the hull were also frustrated because of the weather and the rough seas, which continued to surge in and out of the damaged stern compartments. At one point it was announced that one of the rudders had been freed and it might be possible to make it function, but this was a false hope. A diver by extraordinary exertion had indeed got to the rudder head and detached the coupling, but he found the rudder itself jammed solid. Probably its shaft had been bent out of true. Sometime soon after midnight the engineers gave up the struggle. *Bismarck* could do nothing but wallow slowly through the huge waves directly towards her pursuers, and away from her destination and from any help that might be rendered by friendly ships or aircraft. On deck conditions were appalling. Hitherto she had been steaming before a following wind, so the apparent wind on deck had been almost nil. Now she was moving into wind, and it whistled and shrieked along the decks at 50 knots, tearing at clothing and threatening to hurl men over the side. Even the greenest young seaman must have realised that there was now little hope. Lutjens himself had no doubts at all. At 21.40 hrs he radioed his HQ in Paris: 'Ship unable to manoeuvre. We will fight to the last round, long live the *Führer*!'

All sorts of suggestions have been made as to what might have been done to restore *Bismarck*'s steering. Most of the ideas, such as using a U-boat as a stabiliser, are simply absurd. The only solution that was not tried and might possibly have worked would have been to go astern, using the propellers to steer. This might conceivably have made the ship more manageable, but the reversing turbines were not very powerful, and progress would have been very slow. Even if it had worked, this procedure would not have prevented Tovey from catching up so as to finish the job early on 27 May, just as he eventually did.

Bismarck's armament was still undamaged, and that night the crew proved that they could still fight. Vian's five destroyers, *Cossack*, *Maori*, *Zulu*, *Sikh* and *Piorun* (Polish Navy), were close at hand and determined to make a night attack on the wounded battleship with their torpedoes. Perhaps Tovey remembered how a British destroyer had sunk the battleship *Pomern* at night during the Battle of Jutland. It was clear that with *Sheffield*'s radar out of action *Bismarck* would have to be shadowed during the night and the fast, radar-equipped destroyers were ideal for the task. An aggressive leader like Vian, however, was not going to miss the chance of making an attack at the same time. At this stage no one on the British side knew how badly wounded their opponent really was, and it might well require another torpedo hit to ensure that Rodney and King George V could catch her in the morning. The destroyers rendezvoused with Sheffield, who was able to give them a course for Bismarck, and they steamed towards her in line abreast. The first to make contact was Piorun. She was not in a position to launch a torpedo, but opened-up with her guns, dodging and weaving to avoid the well-aimed salvoes of the enemy. It was a typical display of Polish bravery, but of course, even if she did score any hits, her puny guns would make no difference to a heavily armoured ship. The attackers then worked into position at four corners of a square of which Bismarck was the centre point, with one destroyer directly astern of her. It soon became clear that there was nothing wrong with the enemy's guns or his shooting. German night-sights were far better than British, and the officers in Bismarck's director towers could see the destroyers quite well as they fought through the seas. Six-inch and 15-inch shells straddled them time and again, showering them with splinters and forcing them to haul off. Eventually several of the little ships got their torpedoes off, but fired at long range into the rough seas they had little chance of making a hit. Three torpedoes were fired at 3,000 yards, four at 5,000, three at 6,000, four at 7,000, and two at 9,000. All well beyond safe torpedo range. Also, they were almost certainly set to run at twenty feet, and in the prevailing conditions they might well have passed clean under the target, even if the aim had been good.

At about 02.30 hrs Tovey signalled Vian to start firing star shell so as to indicate Bismarck's position to the approaching battleships. The star-shell attracted yet more violent and accurate fire from the enemy, and the destroyers soon gave up this dangerous activity. They temporarily lost contact with the enemy, but this was not considered a serious problem, as she was clearly disabled and moving very slowly – at about 7 knots – into wind, and would be easy enough to find again. She was actually spotted again by the destroyers at about 05.30, shortly before dawn, and thereafter a close watch was maintained. That Vian's force had not scored a single torpedo hit, in spite of eighteen attempts, was due to the vigorous and accurate fire laid down by *Bismarck*. Vian was convinced that the Germans must have had radar gunlaying to shoot so well at night, but they did not. Mullenheim-Rechberg, who was stationed in the after fire-control station, remembered that he could clearly see the attackers in the darkness through his director sight. For *Bismarck* accurate fire was made difficult by the ship's erratic heading: at one moment the portside guns would bear on a particular target, a few seconds later it was the starboard side guns only. Under these conditions the skill and resolve of the German seamen on their doomed ship deserves the highest praise.

It was a ghastly night for *Bismarck*'s crew. Lindemann attempted to cheer them by broadcasting messages from Paris. These promised that eight U-boats, four Condor aircraft, eighty-one Junkers Ju 88 bombers and an assortment of supply ships and tugs were on the way, and orders were given to send out homing signals so that these forces could find *Bismarck* quickly. There were various heart-warming exhortations from Germany also. Later it was announced that the Spanish cruiser *Canarias* and two destroyers were on the way and would stand by. But any lift given to morale was soon overcome by the appalling weather – it was now blowing at Force 8–9 – and the obvious helplessness of the ship quickly swamped any optimism. From time to time the engines stopped altogether – once because a shaft seized up solid, and several times for other, unexplained reasons. They were still 400 miles from safety and had been at action stations, in many cases, for four days. Utter exhaustion and a feeling of hopelessness set in.

At this point Lütjens determined that he must get his war diary home to Germany. He seems to have felt desperately that some explanation of his strange actions during the operation were fully understood in the Fatherland, and that Raeder was made thoroughly aware of the capability of British radar and its implications for future surface-raiding operations. The only way open to him of getting the diary home was to use one of the Arado float-planes. The precious document was carefully packed and the plane made ready on its catapult; the lucky crew of the Arado were expected to be the only survivors to escape

113

dry-shod from *Bismarck*. The engine started and the order to launch was given, but nothing happened. There seemed to be some fault with the catapult, possibly caused by the last of *Prince of Wales*'s shells. The plane was unceremoniously dumped over the side. Lutjens then sent urgent messages asking for a U-boat to collect the diary. As we have seen, the only boat nearby, *U.556*, was short of fuel and had by now turned for home. *U.74* was the nearest operational boat, and she was instructed to try to collect the document, but weather and enemy destroyers made this impossible. She could make no headway into the storm and remained well clear of the action.

As daylight dawned on 27 May, the British prepared for their final attack. *Rodney* and *King George V* had been looking anxiously for the star-shell bursts fired by the destroyers, but rain squalls had obscured them. Neither the battleships nor the destroyers had been able to take a sun sight for several days, and so they were not too sure of their position, resulting in some desperate, fruitless searching in the wrong place. Time was lost and fuel consumed as Tovey's battleships and the destroyers searched for the enemy and for each other. The problem was solved by *Norfolk*. She had dashed north to try to intercept *Bismarck* when it was supposed that she was heading back towards Iceland, and then, realising the mistake, turned round and steamed towards where she thought the action might be. Wake-Walker was determined to be in at the kill. All of a sudden *Norfolk* found herself dangerously close to an unknown battleship, which turned out to be *Bismarck*. As she sheered away, *Norfolk* caught sight of *Rodney* and *King George V*, and rapidly signalled them to report her contact.

At the same time Somerville was preparing to send another strike from *Ark Royal*. The weather had been bad the day before, but it was worse today. Twice take-off was postponed, but eventually they could wait no longer. It was only with the greatest difficulty that the aircraft were got on deck. Just twelve Swordfish were still serviceable, and these were held in position by extra crews and then lashed down on deck. It was impossible to unfold their wings and position them for take-off as the wind over the deck was too strong, but Captain Maund had another plan. Putting his helm right over, he turned his ship downwind so that the apparent wind on deck was manageable. The turn in those terrible seas made *Ark Royal* dig the sides of her flight-deck into the sea as she rolled, and one Swordfish briefly broke loose, but in the end all was well. The aircraft were prepared for take-off and lashed again to the deck. *Ark Royal* turned upwind again, and the Swordfish, loaded with the last of the stock of torpedoes, staggered off into the gale. They hoped to finish the job they had so brilliantly started the previous day.

As Tovey closed in for the finale, he instructed *Rodney* to conform in general to his movements, but otherwise to take whatever action she thought best. Dalrymple-Hamilton, that independent spirit, would probably have done what he wanted anyway, and as it was he interpreted the admiral's instructions pretty liberally. Tovey was a believer in the so-called 'end-on' approach to the enemy, attacking on a head-to-head course. *Rodney* opted for a more oblique approach, perhaps partly because she could not fire her guns straight ahead without risking damaging her own hull with the recoil of her great guns. As the battleships approached *Bismarck* they realised that, wounded as she was, their task might not be entirely simple. Deprived of most of their destroyer escort, the British ships were dangerously close to enemy U-boat bases, and had to keep steaming fast and changing course often to guard against submarine attack. *Bismarck*'s slow, erratic progress meant that they would have to keep weaving and turning around to remain in a position to use their armament effectively while still maintaining high speed. Also, they were in danger from the air. Already Condor aircraft had been sighted near the fleet, and soon bombers must follow. Into the bargain, the enemy was by no means finished. As far as anyone knew, *Bismarck*'s guns were still undamaged, and she had already proved how effectively she could use them. Worst of all there was the fuel situation. Unless *Bismarck* was sunk well before midday, neither *King George V* nor *Rodney* would have a chance of getting home at a safe speed, as they would simply run out of fuel. Any sea battle so close to enemy-held naval bases is fraught with danger and difficulty, and this was no exception. Tovey could not risk using *Renown* to join the fight, much to her crew's disappointment; she had to remain with *Ark Royal* to protect her from a possible enemy destroyer strike, or from the guns of either of the German heavy ships which he believed still might sortie from Brest. He did have two other useful ships, however. *Norfolk* was already in contact with the enemy, as we have seen. Now another 8-inch cruiser, *Dorsetshire*, normally a part of Force H, had recently joined the hunt, steaming up at maximum speed from convoy escort duty.

At 08.45 on 27 May, both British battleships sighted *Bismarck* at a range of about twelve miles, and *Rodney*'s massive 16-inch guns opened fire a few minutes later. (A plan of this action is given on page 117.) Less that a minute afterwards *King George V* fired her first salvo. *Bismarck* replied almost immediately. Only her forward turrets would bear, and even these were hampered by her erratic course. 'Fifty-five seconds to impact', announced Tovey's gunnery officer, as he saw the flashes of *Bismarck*'s first salvo. The admiral shut him up. 'I don't want to know', he said, 'exactly when a 15-inch shell is going to hit me in the stomach.' High in the anti-aircraft director tower of *Rodney*, Lieutenant Campbell was in a position to watch the fall of shot, undistracted by any enemy aircraft. He was able to see the actual shells clearly, both incoming and outgoing. Horrified, he saw two of his ship's salvoes wide of the target: probably the gunnery officer had overestimated her speed. The third was close but a little short, and at the same time he watched the incoming 15-inch German shells hit the sea just short of *Rodney*, drenching her with water. The second salvo fell close astern, and the third was a perfect straddle, falling on each side of the old ship and sending lethal splinters whizzing round Campbell's director tower. There was nothing wrong with the enemy's shooting. The splinters did no damage until a young sailor picked up one of them and yelled in pain, his hands badly burnt. But that was the last effective resistance from *Bismarck*'s forward turrets. Almost at the same moment a direct hit from *Rodney*'s fourth salvo destroyed 'Bruno', the higher of the two forward turrets, and a few seconds later 'Anton', its partner, went the same way, exploding into a blazing ruin. The same salvo destroyed her central fire-control director. Campbell watched as it went spinning through the air 'like a dustbin lid', streaming smoke and flame and taking its unfortunate occupants

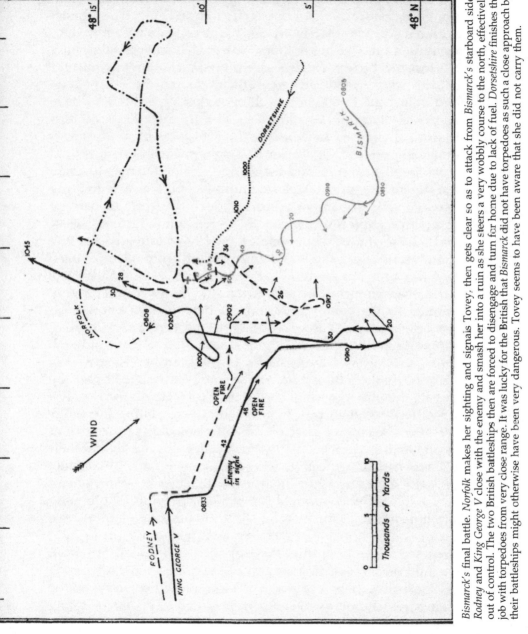

Bismarck's final battle. *Norfolk* makes her sighting and signals Tovey, then gets clear so as to attack from *Bismarck's* starboard side. *Rodney* and *King George V* close with the enemy and smash her into a ruin as she steers a very wobbly course to the north, effectively out of control. The two British battleships then are forced to disengage and turn for home due to lack of fuel. *Dorsetshire* finishes the job with torpedoes from very close range. It was lucky for the British that *Bismarck* did not have torpedoes as such a close approach by their battleships might otherwise have been very dangerous. Tovey seems to have been aware that she did not carry them.

to the sea bottom with it. *Rodney* had altered course to port, which was towards the enemy's track, and it allowed her to bring the full force of her broadside to bear, now firing almost horizontally into the enemy. *King George V*, as yet unfired at, continued on a head-on course towards *Bismarck*, using only her forward turrets. She was steaming directly downwind, and cordite smoke made it very difficult to see the fall of shot and adjust the range, but as she got closer her 14-inch shells began to slam into *Bismarck* also. Shortly after *Rodney*'s turn to port, another barrage opened up. This was from *Bismarck*'s dogged opponent *Norfolk*. She had been in the hunt longer than any other British ship, and she was determined to help to finish the job. *Rodney* was now closing rapidly, and was able to bring her secondary armament to bear. Under a concentrated barrage from three ships, fire from *Bismarck*'s remaining turrets, 'Casar' and 'Dora', started to become erratic but continued for a few minutes. By 09.02 she was being hit hard from all directions, and was little but a wreck.

Rodney then turned herself right round onto a course roughly parallel to the enemy and continued to batter her, now at very close range. This was decidedly not conforming to *King George V*'s movements, as Dalrymple-Hamilton had been ordered, but it certainly was the best way of disabling the enemy. *King George V* had continued on course until she was well past the target, thereby exposing herself to fire from *Bismarck*'s still operational after turrets. Just as these were getting the range the after fire-control director was hit also, and the turrets had to aim and fire independently. In practice this meant that their fire was totally ineffective. Soon *Bismarck*'s resistance virtually ceased. One or two guns managed a few closing shots, one of which landed uncomfortably close to *Rodney*, but as a fighting machine the great ship was finished. Lindemann seems to have given up hope early that morning and made no effort to issue orders or control the ship. Probably he was in utter despair at the mishandling (as he thought) of the mission by Lutjens. He was still alive, however, and was last reported standing on the stem and saluting as the ship went down. (This last sighting may well be imaginary.) Lutjens was probably killed by the shellfire, but in any case neither he nor any of his staff. had any control over the ship or her crew. It appears that only Oels, the executive officer, and some of the engineer officers below, maintained much control of the crewmen around them and continued to issue coherent orders. Internal communications had mostly broken down, but Oels attempted to get men to carry the wounded on deck, and finally gave the order to abandon ship. Mullenheim-Rechberg has asserted that someone ordered that scuttling charges should be set to sink the ship, but there is no way of knowing whether this was done, and if it was done they do not seem to have been effective.

Now for Tovey it was only a question of finally sinking her. At first the two British battleships continued firing at very close range, only about 1,500 yards. This did terrible damage to the enemy's upper works, and killed hundreds of her crew, and men were seen running to and fro in panic and jumping into the water, only to be smashed to pieces as the Atlantic waves hurled them against the steel sides of the ship. A great fire raged below decks and the engine-room crews abandoned their stations, men huddled together wherever they found a place that seemed to be a refuge from the shells. No one seems to have thought of striking the battle ensign and surrendering the ship, which might have saved many lives, and Tovey had no alternative to destroying *Bismarck* utterly. This grisly task was not proving easy, as *King George V*'s guns were now experiencing the same problems as had beset *Prince of Wales*, and both she and *Rodney* were desperately short of fuel. Tovey would have to find other means to finish the job.

Like many old battleships, *Rodney* had an underwater torpedo flat, and in an attempt to finish the unequal battle she fired a series of torpedoes at *Bismarck*. At least one of these scored a hit – the only occasion in history of one battleship torpedoing another – but to no avail. By 10.00 hrs the battered hulk still refused to sink, and the British battleships had to depart for home, leaving the wreck still floating behind them. At this point *Dorsetshire* took a hand; she closed the defenceless hulk and fired two torpedoes, one into each side. The gallant battleship rolled over and sank. Captain Martin, the commander of *Dorsetshire*, had made this final attack entirely on his own initiative and without orders. Oddly enough, a few minutes after he had done it he received an order from Tovey telling him to use torpedoes to finish the enemy off.

We left *Ark Royal*'s Swordfish struggling to get airborne with the last of their torpedoes. As they arrived over the scene of the battle they saw that they had come too late. Shell fire from the friendly ships made it impossible to attempt a torpedo attack, so they were reduced to watching the appalling spectacle of the enemy ship in her death throes. Hundreds of men struggled helpless in the water, many of them limbless or otherwise badly wounded, and being flung about in the gale. As the hull rolled over and sank, hundreds were battered by wreckage or sucked down with the ship. The men who had done so much to bring about this fearful human tragedy were sickened by what they were witnessing. They returned to *Ark Royal* frustrated that they had not been allowed to finish the job themselves (although how they would have done this with their puny 18-inch torpedoes is difficult to imagine), and disgusted by the waste of human life and the suffering they had been unfortunate enough to have to observe. In spite of their magnificent performance on the previous day, there was no feeling of triumph or elation – simply pity for those poor men in the water. There is a story that the Swordfish actually signalled *King George V* and asked her to stop firing so that the aircraft could make their final attack, and that as they did so *King George V*'s ack-ack guns opened fire on them. 'Can't you see them waving?' yelled an officer, 'Those are our own aircraft.' 'Sorry,' was the reply, 'we thought they were Germans shaking their fists.' Evidence for this event, however, is scant, and it is probably imaginary.

Just as the Swordfish landed on *Ark Royal*, the *Luftwaffe* made a belated and inglorious appearance. A Heinkel III appeared out of the clouds, dropped a stick of bombs some distance from *Ark Royal* and hurried off back to France. Force H turned around and steamed back for Gibraltar.

To *Dorsetshire* fell the task of picking up survivors. The sea was covered by a film of heavy, stinking oil and was so rough that it was difficult for survivors to see the cruiser as she lay trying to make a lee, with lines let down and a Carley float alongside. It was difficult to get hold of the slippery lines, and

120

many men fell back into the water exhausted. Out of a total complement of 2,200, 110 men had been rescued when the effort was suddenly abandoned. Someone on *Dorsetshire* thought he had seen a trace of a U-boat nearby (it was imaginary), and Captain Martin decided he must move off. The destroyer *Maori* had also been engaged in picking up survivors, and she followed the cruiser into the distance.

This was a controversial decision, as there were many men still alive in the water, and in any case even U-boat captains would often not attack a vessel engaged in rescuing survivors. Martin, however, had little choice. A stationary cruiser would make a juicy target for a U-boat, and the commander might easily not know what she was doing, especially if the submarine approached from the weather side. He had the safety of his own crew to think about as well as the men in the water, and if there was really a U-boat around she could surely be relied upon to pick up survivors. In fact *U.74*, the only one anywhere near at the time, did briefly sight a ship through her periscope, which was probably *Dorsetshire*, at 10,000 metres – well outside torpedo range. The weather conditions prevented her from closing, and it was far too rough for torpedoes to be expected to run true when fired from on the surface at long range. She did manage to pick up three men in a rubber dinghy. *U.74* was later joined by *U.73* and *U.48*, and they cruised through the oil slick left by the sunken ship but found no one else alive. *Sachenwald*, a weather ship, returning to port to refuel, was also diverted to the scene and managed to find another dinghy with two exhausted survivors. *Canarias*, the Spanish cruiser from Ferrol, also arrived and searched the wreckage but found only corpses.

The passage home for the battleships was not without danger. They were so short of fuel that they had to steam at reduced speed and so were extremely vulnerable to air attack and to U-boats. Also, they were dangerously short of destroyer escorts. Sure enough, in the afternoon of 27 May, after the weather had cleared, 128 aircraft from airfields in France launched three strikes at the returning ships. Two of the destroyers, *Tarta* and *Mashona*, had stayed with *Rodney* until the last possible moment during her action against *Bismarck* and were consequently extremely short of fuel. In order to eke it out on the passage home they had to steam very slowly, and were overtaken by the battleships on their way back to Britain. These destroyers were consequently the first ships found by the strike force, and the full weight of the air assault fell upon them. *Mashona* was sunk, but *Tarta* was able to take advantage of a lull in the attack to pick up most of her crew. In the end, forty-seven men were lost out of a total of 218 on board. In fact the destroyers probably diverted the aircraft from their proper mission, which was to attack the battleships, whose loss would of course have been far more serious than that of *Mashona*.

This was not to be the end of the story. Operation Rhine Exercise had called for no fewer than seven supply ships to be located in Arctic and Atlantic waters to resupply the battleships and cruisers. These ships communicated using a simplified version of the Enigma code, and this could now be read by Bletchley Park. The ships' location signals were transmitted to cruisers operating in the Atlantic, and all seven of them were sunk in short order. Incredibly, neither these sinkings nor the increasing casualty rates soon to be suffered by U-boats led the Germans to consider the possibility that their codes had been broken. Even Dönitz, perhaps the toughest and most intellectually rigorous of the Nazi commanders, simply refused to consider the possibility that the codes had been broken. An intensified hunt was launched for traitors at home, and when none were identified bad luck was blamed.

In Germany the loss of *Bismarck* was seen as an unmitigated disaster. Hitler was justifiably furious. Had he not warned of the danger from enemy aircraft carriers? Had he not instructed that Rhine Exercise should be called off or postponed? How was it possible that even after being detected by British cruisers Lutjens had continued with a plan that depended entirely on surprise? What possible justification could there be for failing to follow up the victory over *Hood* by letting *Prince of Wales* escape? Had Lutjens sunk her and returned home he would have scored a massive and heroic naval victory. Raeder faced the full force of the screaming rage of the *Fuhrer*. Never again would surface raiders be allowed into the Atlantic, and the Grand Admiral had altogether lost what little influence in high places he had ever enjoyed. He continued in his post until January 1943, when in another screaming rage Hitler ordered that the whole surface fleet should be decommissioned, forcing his retirement in favour of Dönitz.

CHAPTER 8

Analysis

If we discount the inconclusive brushes between British and
Italian warships in the Mediterranean, this was the first action
between battleships of any nation since the Battle of Jutland
in May 1916. While the improvements in warship design had
been evolutionary during the intervening twenty-five years,
the developments in aviation had been revolutionary. Neither
Britain nor Germany had fully appreciated the implications of
this for naval warfare, and both were far behind the developments in technology and strategic thinking as regards naval
aviation that had been made in the USA and Japan. The ferocious
naval campaigns that were to be waged in the Pacific from 1942
onwards were entirely dominated by air power. In this context
it is extraordinary that on the German side aircraft played
almost no part in the action or in the plans for it. The side with
the most effective air arm won this battle and was to win almost
every naval engagement in the Second World War. The outcome of the *Bismarck* episode was determined by the ability of
Britain to deploy its air power effectively. This is the overall
conclusion reached by both sides. After it, Britain worked hard
to improve her Fleet Air Arm and Coastal Command, and even
Germany briefly restarted work on the carrier *Graf Zeppelin*,
and began training a squadron of Ju 87 (Stuka) crews in deck
landing. Soon the demands of the Russian campaign called
a halt to the work on the carrier, but oddly enough the Stukas

continued their training until quite late in the war. Maybe every-one had forgotten about them.

It is interesting to examine how the two naval staffs per-formed in the contest, and to examine how the strengths and weaknesses of the key players affected the outcome. On the British side the hunt for *Bismarck* was handled at the highest levels of the government. Churchill fancied himself as a naval strategist, which he certainly was not. He spent many hours during the hunt in conference in the Admiralty, egging on Sir Dudley Pound, the First Sea Lord, and Sir Thomas Phillips, the Vice-Chief of the Naval Staff, as they directed the chase. His powerful presence completely dominated the assembled com-pany, and his constant nagging caused far too many signals to be sent to ships at sea. This torrent of advice, admonition, instructions and inaccurate information made the work of the admirals and captains at sea doubly difficult. Pound was com-pletely incapable of controlling him, and Phillips, who was soon to lose two valuable capital ships as well as his own life as a result of his grossly incompetent handling of *Prince of Wales* and *Repulse*'s expedition to the Far East, seems to have actually made things worse. However, it must be said that the Admiralty's strategy in intercepting *Bismarck* was in essence sound. For all his faults as a naval tactician, Churchill did understand some-thing about air power, having learnt to fly himself when he was First Lord of the Admiralty, and he did not under-estimate the part that carrier-borne aircraft could play in the conflict. He had been one of the earliest champions of the Royal Naval Air Service before and during the First World War.

On the intelligence front, the collection of information from the various sources – Enigma, French and Norwegian resist-ance, aerial reconnaissance and radio direction finding – was excellent, and this was expertly sifted, interpreted and co-ordinated. Especially impressive was the successful disguising of the breaking of Enigma, which was to be of incalculable value throughout the war.

A tactical failure on the part of the Royal Navy was the supply of fuel to the fleet. Whereas Germany (and much later in the war the US Navy) placed great emphasis on having tankers and supply ships in place to support naval operations, the Royal

Navy seems to have been reluctant to undertake resupply and refuelling at sea. This very nearly led to the whole chase having to be called off in its final phase, allowing *Bismarck*, damaged though she was, to escape. A tanker, suitably escorted, in the Western Approaches or even further out into the Atlantic, might have played a key role in allowing ships to stay on station longer and finish the job they had begun. It would also have enabled better use to have been made of the destroyers available, for most of these spent far too much of their time steaming back and forth to Iceland to refuel.

Unlike generals, who are normally situated safely well behind the front line, admirals in the Second World War were frequently at sea and faced the same dangers as ordinary seamen. In fact, as we have seen, two of them, Holland and Lutjens, were killed in the *Bismarck* episode. Of the British admirals Tovey emerged as an excellent leader and tactician. When the breakout was first discovered he resisted the temptation to close off any options, or to dash off to sea with no idea where to go, and he quickly marshalled all the assets available, including *Victorious*, the invaluable *Rodney*, and destroyers from far and wide. He also showed that he had learnt lessons from the disappointing (from the British point of view) outcomes of the Battle of Jutland. He waited until daylight before employing his overwhelmingly superior forces against his crippled enemy and he insisted that she should be finally sunk. At Jutland the German battle cruiser *Seydlitz* had been hit by at least one torpedo, and smashed over and over again by heavy gunfire. She was so full of water that her decks, like those of *Bismarck*, were awash, but, again like *Bismarck*, her engines would still turn. She limped home and was repaired. Unless he actually saw her sink, Tovey was right not to halt his attack on his enemy, however battered she might seem to be. It has been suggested that his tactic of approaching his enemy head-on, in a position that made it impossible for him to use his broadside in the opening stages of the engagement, was wrong. Actually it was a tactic to which he had given a great deal of thought, and he believed it correct. He had observed that most misses by heavy guns were not 'overs' or 'shorts', but to the left or right of the target. Thus the practice of approaching an enemy head-on minimised the chance of being hit because it presented only the relatively narrow beam of one's own ship to the enemy's fire. In practice it seemed to work. *Bismarck's* superb gunnery team failed to score a single hit on *King George V* or *Rodney*. Another factor was that the extraordinary configuration of *Rodney's* turrets made it difficult for her to use her broadside effectively, and impossible for her to shoot at a target much aft of abeam. An oblique head-on approach was ideal for her. Tovey knew her particularly well, having been her captain in the early 1930s. One of the major British errors made during the pursuit was the navigational mix-up that led *King George V* and her companions to steam in almost exactly the wrong direction for seven hours. It was Tovey's navigation officer who made the mistake, and Tovey must take the blame for such a blunder by his staff, but this is almost the only criticism which can be levelled at him.

Somerville emerges from the affair as an outstanding leader and an excellent seaman. It was his leadership and insistence on intensive flying training for his crews that gave them the confidence and the commitment to operate in weather conditions that were theoretically impossible for flying. More than that, the mechanics, riggers, seamen and deck officers on *Ark Royal* had been welded together into a team by his example and his inspiration. Under him men 'knew they could do the impossible and went on and did it.' The only major mistake by his Force H was the accidental attack on *Sheffield*, due to an overload of work in *Ark Royal's* signal office, which prevented a message being passed on to the flight crews before they took off. It is a little hard to blame this on Somerville. He also showed great courage and not a little ingenuity in proposing his scheme for using *Renown's* gunfire under cover of smoke to attack *Bismarck* from upwind. It was probably lucky that the tactic never had to be attempted, but the suggestion itself is a great tribute to the bravery of the man whose own battle station was high above *Renown's* bridge. He would have had little chance of surviving the action.

Rear Admiral Wake-Walker, who commanded the Arctic Patrol consisting of *Norfolk* and *Suffolk*, carried out his shadowing role very competently. It is easy to forget today how novel and temperamental radar was in those early days, and his use of it, combined with the cover of the fog banks, was masterly. He also took under his command *Prince of Wales* after the sinking of *Hood*, and used her effectively to harry his adversary without exposing herself to too much danger. He has been criticised for not becoming involved in the Battle of the Denmark Strait, but, as we have seen, he was not really in a position to do so and had no orders from Admiral Holland. Blame for the loss of contact by *Suffolk* can perhaps be laid at his door. Had the cruisers not been zigzagging, this loss probably would not have happened. Wake-Walker ordered the zigzagging because he had had a specific warning of U-boats in the area, and he followed what was standard procedure when such a danger threatened. It does seem, however, that he was being a little over-cautious. The cruisers were travelling at about 27 knots in bad visibility and it is unlikely that a U-boat would have got a chance of a successful shot at such a fast-moving target. In view of the vital necessity of keeping contact with *Bismarck*, it would have been a wise decision to keep on a straight course astern of her. He certainly showed no lack of aggression in the final stages of the battle when he provided the vital link between the British battleships and their quarry, and engaged *Bismarck* effectively with his own guns.

Bowhill, in command of RAF Coastal Command, has never received the plaudits he deserves for his contribution to the Battle of the Atlantic or to the *Bismarck* hunt. Britain was indeed lucky that men of his calibre and experience survived the First World War and were in senior positions in 1939.

Vice-Admiral Holland, however, on board *Hood*, made a series of errors that are hard to understand, because Holland had a reputation as an intelligent and expert naval tactician. Yet he failed to keep his force together, thus depriving himself of the advantage given him by his destroyers. These could have been decisive in the subsequent action. He seems to have utterly ignored the presence of *Norfolk* and *Suffolk* and their potential to distract the enemy and influence the battle. It was not his fault that he missed *Bismarck* during the night, as this difficulty was caused by *Suffolk*'s temporary loss of contact coinciding with *Bismarck*'s slight alteration of course. Once contact had been re-established, however, it was mad to approach such a powerful enemy from aft of the beam in a position where only his forward guns could bear and his enemies could deploy their whole broadsides effectively, 'crossing his tee'. This approach also exposed *Hood* to the very thing that was likely to be fatal to her – long-range plunging shots smashing through her weak deck armour. And why was *Hood* in the lead? *Prince of Wales*'s crew was certainly green and her guns were in poor shape, but at least she was heavily armoured and could have stood up to enemy fire far better than *Hood*. She could also have used her radar to locate and engage the enemy before she herself was seen. Situated as she was, astern of *Hood*, she could not do this, and indeed she was ordered to switch her radar off altogether 'in case it gave their position away'. Unlike Tovey's orders to *Rodney* to conform generally to the admiral's movements, Leach on *Prince of Wales* was instructed to follow his chief's lead precisely, and so he had no scope for independent action. The unfortunate Holland, who had in fact had no previous battle experience, seems to have lost his powers of reasoning completely when confronted by an actual battle situation.

In spite of shortcomings at the Admiralty and of one of the admirals on the spot, the *Bismarck* chase showed that at least at lower levels in the service officers had learnt from the failures of the Royal Navy in the First World War. At Jutland, and in the North Sea engagements which preceded it, captains of ships considered it their duty to follow their admiral at all costs, to use no independent thought whatever and not even bother to report what they knew on enemy movements. This wooden follow-my-leader approach resulted in lack-lustre performance and total failure to achieve victory, even when it was virtually handed to them on a plate. Second World War captains were made of different stuff. Dalrymple-Hamilton ignored instructions that he thought to be wrong so that he could be sure of bringing his ship into action, and then, when the battle was to be fought, handled his ship very effectively in his own way, with scant regard to orders. He also showed himself an inspirational leader, motivating his engine-room team to keep the tired old ship steaming at full speed in spite of worn-out engines and boilers. Bovell of *Victorious* also showed an independent spirit, refusing to risk the lives of his flight crews by turning off his searchlights. Vian, although ordered to join Tovey, turned towards *Bismarck* to make his night attacks initially without orders. Maund's downwind turn to enable aircraft to be readied on deck was entirely contrary to accepted practice, but it worked well. He also authorised the unconventional settings and fusing of the torpedoes. Martin, aboard *Dorsetshire*, gave the enemy the *coup de grâce* on his own initiative. At this level at least the lessons of the First World War had been well learnt.

As we have seen, radar played a vital part in the battle, and in this branch of technology Britain was undoubtedly the world leader. Not only was the technology the most advanced, but also the training in its use at sea seems to have been well handled. The Germans not only had inferior equipment, but they also failed to make it robust enough for shipboard service, and as a result their gun-director teams seem to have been reluctant to use it. British planning and technology development between the wars had been pathetically inadequate in many spheres, but this one vital area compensated for many shortcomings elsewhere.

On the German side, strategy was flawed from the start. The Germans depended on the excellent quality of their equipment and the superb skill and fighting spirit of their men to make up for some very shoddy planning.

Hitler himself realised that he knew nothing of sea warfare. He gave warnings about the potential of air power and the dangers of the mission, but then left the navy well alone. It was to prove unfortunate for Germany that he did not show the same restraint in the land war.

Raeder performed badly by any standards. He allowed the internal rivalries within the Nazi regime to push him into launching Rhine Exercise with one battleship and a heavy cruiser when the original intention was to have two large battleships and two other powerful heavy ships. *Bismarck*'s crew fought bravely and their gunnery was excellent, but realistically their chances of success in the north Atlantic, in the face of a vastly superior British fleet, were small. Lutjens was right to protest about the policy of using the surface fleet 'in teaspoonfuls'. All sound military and naval strategy depends on concentrating force and using it at the right moment, not when it happens to be politically convenient. Raeder had three opportunities to call off the operation and cut his losses. He could have done this when Hitler suggested that the force should be recalled while it was still in Norwegian waters, when it had been detected by the cruisers in the Denmark Strait and had thus lost any chance of surprise, or after the battle with *Hood* and *King George V*. He took none of them. The loss of *Bismarck* was largely due to the Grand Admiral's misjudgement, and this was quite clearly understood by Hitler. Raeder remained in post until early 1943, when he was finally dismissed, but in reality his hands were tied as soon as *Bismarck* was lost. His policy of using the surface fleet in the Atlantic was finally abandoned when the capital ships were withdrawn from the French ports in February 1942. A particular weakness of Raeder's which affected Operation Rhine Exercise was his failure to mount combined operations with the *Luftwaffe*. One of the essential features of naval warfare in the Second World War was that almost any operation had to be a combined effort using seaborne and airborne assets. Raeder had no aircraft of his own, and was not politician enough to procure the wholehearted support of Göring and his powerful *Luftwaffe*. Göring himself jealously defended anything that could fly from the influence of all other arms, and so there were no German aircraft specifically designed to support long-range naval operations. Raeder was constantly getting the brush-off from the *Luftwaffe* command. He failed to get control of the Condor aircraft based in France and used exclusively on anti-shipping missions. He pressed hard for the long-range Heinkel He 117 to be made available to support U-boat and surface-ship operations, but Göring refused to co-operate. Even the float-planes carried on the warships were flown by *Luftwaffe* crews who reported ultimately to their own commanders, not the *Kriegsmarine*. There appears to have been little inter-service planning at any stage during Rhine Exercise, and the *Luftwaffe* seems to have made only feeble efforts to give *Bismarck* support or cover; there was, in fact, no concept of a 'joint operation'. The navy, for example, was not informed about air operations over their route past the Danish islands. The reconnaissance flown over Scapa was botched and the fighter patrol over the anchorage near Bergen failed to spot Suckling's high-flying Spitfire.

Worst of all, no cover was given while *Bismarck* was being attacked by *Ark Royal*'s Swordfish. Germany possessed long-range twin-engined fighters, the Junkers Ju 88Cs, which had a range of 1,700 miles. These could have flown from bases in France and harried the Swordfish on their crucial attack mission. The weather was bad but by no means impossible. Had there been a proper joint planning exercise, the Ju 88s could have been made available and turned the tables on the Fleet Air Arm. But Raeder, stiff, reserved and haughty, was not one to win friendly co-operation from the likes of Göring. Only when the *Bismarck* was lost and there seemed to be some chance of scoring a propaganda success where the *Kriegsmarine* had failed did the *Luftwaffe* launch a formidable air fleet to attack the returning British ships. Justifying his decisions after the war, Raeder wrote:

Whether or not to send *Bismarck* out presented me with an extraordinarily difficult problem ... some of the thinking on the subject no longer obtained. The sortie of *Bismarck* was to have been a part of a broad operational plan, but now if she went out it would be an individual undertaking and there was a possibility that the enemy would concentrate his forces against her. That seriously increased the risk. On the other hand the military situation was such that we could not afford simply to conserve such a powerful combatant. Postponing the operation until *Scharnhorst* and *Gneisenau* were again ready for sea might mean that we would never be able to use the new battleship for operations in the Atlantic. It was almost impossible to predict when *Scharnhorst* and *Gneisenau*, which lay in port in northern France and were subject to constant attacks by the RAF, would be combat ready. In fact neither ship was ready for sea until February 1942. Postponing the action still further until *Tirpitz* was ready for action would result in at least a year and a half of inactivity – a period during which the enemy would not be inactive, and the situation in the Atlantic would probably deteriorate further because of the attitude of the United States, if for no other reason.

An extremely strong psychological ground for my decision was the confidence I had in the leadership of Admiral Lutjens, an officer who understood sea warfare inside out ... The decision to give the final order to carry out the operation was made very much more difficult for me by Hitler's attitude. When I informed him of my plans he did not reject them, but it was evident that he was not in complete agreement with them. He left the decision up to me. At the beginning of May he had a long conversation in Gotenhafen with Admiral Lutjens, who described his experiences of the Atlantic cruises of *Scharnhorst* and *Gneisenau* and explained the intentions for the tactical deployment of *Bismarck*. He also pointed out the serious danger which enemy aircraft carriers presented for the battleship.

After carefully weighing all the circumstances I gave the order to go ahead.

This is a revealing statement, as it shows clearly how pressure to do something with the ships at his disposal overrode his normal sound judgement. The mind set which says, 'We must use these ships because we have got them', is inevitably fatal to proper planning. Perhaps the penultimate sentence also reveals Lutjens's state of mind before his mission and points to an attempt to derail the whole enterprise.

Lutjens himself remains an enigmatic figure. Unless explained by some private agenda his actions in not refuelling, in allowing *Prince of Wales* to escape and in sending too many long radio transmissions seem downright irresponsible. One can imagine that had he not been on board, *Bismarck* under Lindemann would have sunk *Prince of Wales* as well as *Hood*, and returned to Germany in triumph. Maybe it was, as Mullenheim-Rechberg has suggested, a mental breakdown of some kind, or maybe he did have his own agenda. The truth will never be known, but it is impossible to deny that this previously capable and undoubtedly brave officer performed extraordinarily badly on this occasion.

Other German officers involved behaved with the competence and vigour always associated with the German navy. Lindemann was clearly a well-liked and highly respected captain, and the excellent gunnery performance displayed by both *Bismarck* and *Prinz Eugen* is an eloquent testament to the efficiency of the training they had been given and to the discipline of the crews. This was displayed brilliantly in the battle with *Hood* and *Prince of Wales*, and with astonishing fortitude in the night battle with the destroyers. Oels, *Bismarck's* executive officer, in particular seems to have radiated calm and efficiency even when the ship was in her death throes. It was his example, at least in part, that ensured that she kept fighting until she was no more than a wreck.

Having said this, two areas of criticism can be identified in *Bismarck's* performance. Firstly her engineering staff seem to have had more difficulty than might have been expected in recovering the 1,000 tons of fuel oil from the damaged forward tanks. There were many associated problems, but it is difficult not to believe that even in heavy weather, a team who knew their ship well and were sufficiently resourceful could have devised a more rapid and effective solution than that which was eventually able to recover a few last dregs. More oil recovered would have enabled the ship to steam faster and could have had a critical effect on the outcome. The other fault was with the anti-aircraft gunnery. Even given the cloud conditions, which were ideal for torpedo attack, and the astonishing flying characteristics of the Swordfish, it is amazing that *Bismarck's* AA batteries did not account for a single one of their attackers. This must be attributed to lack of proper training with low-flying targets and to the faulty design of the AA fire-director system. The failure was also partly due to inadequate armament and technology. Warships during the Second World War were almost all inadequate in respect of AA armament, and more and more was constantly being added to them. For example, Iowa Class US battleships had twenty 5-inch and sixty-nine 20 mm AA guns, together with excellent gun-control radar. When engaged in operations, US battleships were invariably supported by an anti-aircraft picket of cruisers and destroyers also fitted with formidable AA batteries. Even so, Japanese aircraft, including kamikazes, were able to get through and damage them. Designed as she was to operate alone in the hostile Atlantic, *Bismarck* should have been given far more medium- and close-range AA armament than she had, and her men should have been properly trained in its use. Germany in 1941 had excellent anti-aircraft radar, but it was not fitted to warships. This represented a serious failure by the *Kriegsmarine* to make use of available technology.

The battle with *Bismarck*, one-sided though it was, was a contest that Britain simply had to win. The U-boats were stretching Britain's resources in men, warships and merchantmen almost to breaking point. Had *Bismarck* succeeded in a foray into the Atlantic, or even in reaching a French port, every convoy would have needed a capital ship escort, and there were just not enough heavy ships to go round. Probably the only course would have been to abandon the Mediterranean and use the handful of serviceable ships there to help to cover Atlantic convoys. This would, of course, have meant surrendering Malta and abandoning our armies in north Africa. Even then, many of the Atlantic convoys would be depending for protection on ancient vessels incapable of putting up much of a fight against a fast modern ship like *Bismarck*. The Home Fleet, one of whose duties it was to make it difficult for German ships to reach the Atlantic, would have been impossibly stretched by convoy activities. It would then have become relatively easy for *Tirpitz* to join *Bismarck*, and the two together would have formed a unit too strong for the Royal Navy to handle with confidence. In short, British command of the sea would have been lost. The political consequences also would have been disastrous. At this point in the war everything was going badly, with defeats in Crete and north Africa, and public opinion in the USA was beginning to believe once again that Britain was incapable of surviving, let alone winning the war. In these circumstances American planning was centring on preventing British ships and aircraft from falling into German hands, not on supporting or joining the fight. The escape of the *Bismarck* and the sinking of *Hood* might have finally decided Roosevelt against any further support for Britain.

The British victory was due primarily to the good co-operation between ships and aircraft, both of the Fleet Air Arm and of the RAF. It was, after all, the RAF that managed to keep *Scharnhorst* and *Gneisenau* out of action when their participation in Rhine Exercise was almost a condition of its viability. It was the RAF that found the quarry after she had been lost, and the Fleet Air Arm whose indomitable spirit and matchless skill disabled her. It was an RAF Spitfire that found her in the fjord and a naval Maryland that confirmed that she had left it. The co-operation between the Royal Navy and Coastal Command of the RAF, dubious at the start of the war, was rapidly improving and was soon to prove decisive in the Battle of the Atlantic. But these achievements by aircraft must not allow us to forget the role played by warships. The two cruisers that found *Bismarck*, and tracked her during her dash for the Atlantic, forced her to undertake her first deadly encounter with British capital ships. During that encounter the fatal shells fired by *Prince of Wales* started the train of events that led to *Bismarck's* destruction. In the end it was only the heavy guns of *Rodney* and *King George V* and torpedoes from the cruisers that could finally destroy her. Also, it must be remembered that the carrier aircraft that proved so formidable could do nothing unless the carriers themselves were properly protected by capital ships and destroyers. The losses of *Courageous* and *Glorious* are sufficient proof of this. A carrier launching and receiving aircraft is particularly vulnerable to attack by aircraft, submarines or enemy capital ships. The great Battle of Midway in the Pacific in 1942 shows clearly how vulnerable carriers could be in these conditions. (The Japanese lost no fewer than four carriers in a few hours, and these carriers had no close heavy-ship escort.) The crucial lesson learnt in the Second World War was that only properly planned combined operations had any chance of success.

Ironically, at the very time when the Royal Navy showed that it had understood this in the *Bismarck* chase, the Germans were inflicting terrible losses on British ships operating without air support around Crete. This débâcle was entirely caused by Churchill's ill-considered adventure into the war in Greece, another example of an operation undertaken for political reasons and without proper combined planning. Even after this, not all senior Royal Navy officers had got the message. *Prince of Wales* and *Repulse* were operating within range of Allied fighters when they were sunk by Japanese aircraft. Admiral Phillips had not seen fit to ask for air cover.

The Germans did learn one clear lesson from the *Bismarck* episode, and Lutjens was perhaps the first to articulate it. Radar had changed the whole balance of sea warfare. No longer could warships hope to lurk unseen in the ocean, pouncing out on some unsuspecting merchantman or lightly escorted convoy and then vanish again into the vastness and the fogs of the North Atlantic. Seaborne or airborne radar could penetrate through the thickest and darkest weather, and sooner or later retribution would fall on the surface raider. This was the message that Lutjens sent over and over again to Berlin, and it was fully understood.

The Allied Russian convoys, as they progressed up the Norwegian coast, close to German air and naval bases, were thus to become the only target outside the Baltic against which Hitler's surviving heavy ships could be used. As long as they were present in the fjords, a substantial part of the Royal Navy had to be kept on standby to deal with them. The best tactic that the Germans could adopt was to maintain them as a threat and not risk them in action, and this was the policy that was in fact eventually adopted. On the rare occasions that the battleships and battle cruisers put to sea they were under such strict orders to avoid combat that they were ineffective. The culmination of this was the Battle of the Barents Sea in December 1942, during which a convoy escorted by the cruisers *Sheffield* and *Jamaica* and a handful of destroyers was attacked by a superior German force, including the pocket battleship *Lutzow* and the heavy cruiser *Hipper*. So strict were Admiral Kummetz's instructions about avoiding damage to his ships that he withdrew as soon as a hit was scored on *Hipper*. This defeat put Hitler into such a rage that he demanded the scrapping of the whole surface fleet and precipitated the resignation of Raeder.

The subsequent history of Hitler's battleships is not glorious. *Bismarck*'s sister ship *Tirpitz* achieved virtually nothing. On her first expedition in January 1942 she attempted an attack on shipping in northern waters but was unsuccessful. In early 1943 she put to sea again, bound for Narvik, and then into the Kaafjord, an inlet forming part of the Altenfjord in northern

Norway. From there she sailed with *Scharnhorst* to Spitzbergen, where she bombarded shore installations while troops were landed to occupy the island. Returning to the Altenfjord, she was attacked by British two-man torpedoes, which did severe damage. Repairs took five months, and no sooner had they been completed than she was hit by bombs from aircraft flown from a carrier force including *Furious* and *Victorious*. She suffered casualties and was again put out of action. In August 1944 she was bombed again, and in September she was fatally damaged by 12,000 lb Tallboy bombs dropped by long-range Lancasters. She was towed into the Kaafjord, where the Germans success- fully disguised her unserviceable condition. A further Lancaster strike was ordered in November, which caused her to capsize and finally sink, taking all but fifty of her crew with her. The only substantial contribution this powerful and costly ship made to the war effort was to tie up British forces monitoring and attacking her.

Scharnhorst was heavily damaged by mines during the Channel Dash in February 1942, but made it first to the Baltic and then to northern waters for the Spitzbergen operation. In December 1943 she put to sea to intercept what appeared to be a lightly escorted convoy off the North Cape, but was ambushed by a strong British force led by the battleship *Duke of York*. Battered by shells and torpedoes, she sank in the icy Arctic Sea on 26 December. *Gneisenau* was decommissioned after being severely damaged during the Channel Dash, and was eventually scrapped. *Lutzow* and *Hipper* participated ingloriously in the Battle of the Barents Sea, *Lutzow* then returning to Germany and eventually being used to help evacuate Germans in front of the Soviet advances. Sunk by bombs in harbour at Swinemunde, her turrets remained above the water and she was used as an artillery battery until a serious fire put her completely out of action and she was blown up by the retreating Germans. *Admiral Scheer*, after her successful voyage to the South Atlantic and the Indian Ocean, returned for a refit, and then operated in the Baltic, seeing very little action. She made an expedition to the Arctic in 1942, but again without any result. Finally she operated again in the Baltic, mainly in an army co-operation role. In April 1945 she ferried 1,000 refugees and wounded from Pillau to Kiel, where she was promptly sunk by Allied bombing.

Thus the sinking of *Bismarck* marked the end of any strategically important employment of the fine surface-ships that Germany had built between the wars. Like the fleet that had existed in 1914, Hitler's seven battleships had little to show for the precious resources of money, skilled labour, men and materials that had been invested in them. It is frightening to contemplate what might have happened if these resources had instead been applied to building and manning submarines.

Organisation of the *Kriegsmarine*

After the First World War and the surrender of the German fleet, draconian restrictions were placed on any future German naval development. The Treaty of Versailles imposed the following limits.

Battleships
6 plus 2 reserve. All modern battleships had to be surrendered, only a few ancient pre-Dreadnoughts were allowed to be retained. No new battleships exceeding 10,000 tons to be built.

Cruisers
6 plus 2 reserve. No new cruisers over 6,000 tons to be built.

Destroyers
12 plus 4 reserve. No new destroyers over 800 tons to be built

Torpedo boats
12 plus 4 reserve. No new torpedo boats over 200 tons to be built

Submarines
None to be either owned or built.

Aircraft carriers
None to be either owned or built.

Naval aviation
Prohibited

Armament on ships was also restricted by the treaty.
In addition the navy was reduced to a maximum of 15,000 men, including 1,500 officers.

The puny force envisaged by these restrictions was rapidly augmented by various devices and subterfuges, especially in the field of submarines (which were built in Holland by an under-cover German operation). Gradually the Allies were persuaded to relax the restrictions, and by the late 1930s Germany was in a position to ignore them completely. One of the effects of the reduction of numbers of personnel was to enable the new *Kriegsmarine* to be extremely selective in who it recruited, and so the quality of senior officers and seamen was exceptionally high. Another effect was that, as almost all the First World War ships were surrendered, completely new and innovative designs could be adopted. As a result, in contrast to Britain, which entered the war with ten battleships laid down before the out-break of the First World War, and even destroyers and sub-marines that were built before 1918, Germany had a chance to start with a completely clean sheet.

The organisation of the Kriegsmarine evolved quite rapidly as more ships came into service, and a further phase of re-organisation took place as the Nordic countries and France fell under Nazi domination. Raeder, the long-term chief of the navy, was a stickler for discipline and obedience, and ruthlessly sacked senior officers who showed any lack of either. Hence senior personnel changes were frequent. By 1941 the command structure in so far as it relates to the *Bismarck* episode was as follows:

Supreme Commander-in-Chief
Adolf Hitler

Supreme Commander-in-Chief Navy
Erich Raeder

Fleet Commander
Gunther Lutjens

Command Group North
Rolf Carls

Command Group West
Alfred Saalwachter

Commander U-boats
Karl Dönitz

This was perhaps an over-complicated, almost top-heavy organisation for a relatively small navy, and in practice did not work well. The Fleet Commander normally sailed with any major expedition of the fleet and was in direct control of the warships involved. The local group commanders, however, were comfortably based in Oslo and Paris. They were responsible for naval operations in northern waters and the north Atlantic respectively, and while the Fleet Commander operated in their areas he was at least in theory under their control. In practice he seems to have taken little notice of them. During the *Bismarck*'s voyage they seem to have done a poor job. The intelligence received from Carls was wrong both as regards the possibility of Swedish reports of the voyage reaching England and later when he reported again that the breakout was undetected after the ships left the Oslo Fjord. Saalwachter seems to have only made token attempts to help *Bismarck* in her last hours. There were powerful ocean-going tugs available to him that might at least have tried to help her, and it seems strange that the destroyers in Brest found it impossible to put to sea. German destroyers of the time were generally bigger and better armed than their British equivalents, and yet the British destroyers of all classes remained at sea and participated in the battle.

The Commander U-boats in theory operated under the same regime as the Fleet Commander, although in practice he exerted almost complete independence. His base was not in Paris but close to his boats, near Lorient. Had he been more fully appraised of the progress of the action and of the Fleet Commander's plans as they developed, he might have been able to make an effective intervention in spite of the bad weather.

The most glaring fault in the German organisation, however, was the lack of any sort of air force involvement. There had been a German naval air arm in the 1920s disguised as a yachting club, and this had trained a few selected naval personnel to fly military aircraft. However, as the Nazi party took control of the nascent *Kriegsmarine*, Göring was able to take over all naval aircraft and some key personnel. Thereafter the navy only got as much help from air operations as the *Reichmarshal* thought fit to provide. This, together with the suspension of all work on the carrier *Graf Zeppelin*, had a seriously damaging effect on surface-ship operations.

Overall one cannot avoid the impression of an organisation with too many admirals, too much politics and too few ships.

The Fleet Air Arm and RAF Coastal Command

The Admiralty became interested in aircraft as early as 1903, when experiments were made with observation kites. In 1907 it was actually offered, for purchase, the Wright Brothers' patents, but declined, preferring lighter-than-air machines at that time. In 1909 Lieutenant Samson flew a Short biplane off the bows of the battleship *Africa*, which was the first shipboard launch of a military aircraft. In 1914 the importance of air operations was recognised by the establishment of the Royal Naval Air Service (RNAS), an organisation totally under the authority of the Royal Navy, and operating seaplanes, land-based machines and later ship-borne wheeled aircraft. By the time war broke out there were two seaplane carriers in commission, and their aircraft were used for various reconnaissance, bombing and anti-airship operations. As early as 1915 the first attempts were made to launch torpedoes from aircraft, and a notable success was achieved by Flight Commander Edmonds, who managed to sink a 5,000-ton Turkish merchant ship using a 14-inch torpedo. The RNAS mounted a successful attack on Zeppelin sheds near Düsseldorf, and less-successful operations against an airship factory on Lake Constance and at Cuxhaven. It also had responsibility for destroying Zeppelins attempting to bomb Britain, and after a shaky start was very successful in this role.

The service and its range of activities increased rapidly, especially in the anti-submarine role, but the relative inactivity of the war at sea enabled the Admiralty to release numbers of trained pilots and observers to assist the army's Royal Flying Corps (RFC) in France and on other fronts. Early in 1918 the government commissioned General Smuts, the South African soldier and statesman, to report on how to make the best use of air power in the war, and he immediately noticed the overlap of activities between the RNAS and the RFC. On 1 April 1918 both forces were merged into an entirely new, separate organisation, the Royal Air Force. No fewer than 55,000 naval officers and ratings, together with 2,500 aircraft, joined this new arm, representing a substantial part of its total strength. Britain was the undisputed world leader in naval aviation.

The end of the war and the era of disarmament that followed reduced the RAF to a shadow of its former self, and no branch suffered more in this than the former RNAS. The RAF was not interested, and the Royal Navy had little regard for the RAF personnel with their separate uniforms, skills and culture, who operated the few obsolete aircraft assigned to them for maritime duties. Britain consequently entirely lost her lead in naval aviation to the USA and Japan.

In 1924 the Balfour Committee was set up to examine this situation, and proposed the establishment of a new entity – the Fleet Air Arm (FAA). This would come under the ultimate control of the RAF but would be manned mainly by naval personnel, the officers holding commissions in both the RAF and the Royal Navy. This somewhat half-baked compromise resulted in a rather unloved force, which nevertheless possessed a number of aircraft carriers and, fortunately, a core of dedicated and highly skilled flyers. It was considered by senior naval officers, however, to be a bit of a backwater. The famous Admiral Cunningham, for example, tore up the application to join the FAA submitted to him by one aspiring aviator. 'No,' he said, 'I am not going to see a good officer's career ruined.' There was, correspondingly, a strong tendency among senior ranks to play down the contribution aircraft could make to naval warfare. Aircraft could perhaps be useful against submarines, and for artillery spotting, but they would never sink a capital ship under way. The very idea was absurd.

It is hardly surprising that the development of specialised aircraft was almost entirely neglected during this sorry phase in the history of British naval aviation. Both the RAF and the Royal Navy had different ideas as to what was required, and neither wanted to pay for the development of new types. A naval aircraft at that time had totally different requirements from conventional aircraft. It needed to be more robust, normally to have a longer endurance, and to have folding wings so as to fit into a small space. Americans and Japanese developed admirable aircraft answering these criteria, but Britain did not. The result was that while the RAF's Fighter Command was dragged into the modern era by visionaries such as Sidney Camm of Hawker and R.J. Mitchell of Supermarine, the FAA was stuck with obsolete biplanes, and a few inadequate underpowered machines such as the Fulmar, Skua and Roc. Particularly unsatisfactory was the absence of any ship-borne fighter capable of giving defence to the fleet when faced with the danger of air attack from well-handled modern aircraft, such as those of the *Luftwaffe*. Eventually this gap had to be filled by imported American fighters. American aircraft such as the Martlet and Avenger were eventually acquired as fighters and strike aircraft.

In 1937 yet another report, this time by Sir Thomas Inskip, recommended that the FAA should be returned to full naval control. This was implemented in so far as ship-borne aircraft were concerned, but maritime reconnaissance and shore-based anti-submarine and strike activity remained the responsibility of the RAF.

The FAA entered the war with some 230 aircraft and 360 pilots – a mere shadow of the force that had existed in 1918. Small, ill equipped, often ignored and frequently reorganised, the service might have been expected to be demoralised and defeatist. In fact the reverse is true. The skill, courage and enterprise that the FAA demonstrated during the war ranks second to none. The *Bismarck* episode is a good example of its indomitable spirit.

If maritime aviation had been the Cinderella of the services before Inskip, the rump left to the RAF after the separation of the FAA was yet more unfortunate. By 1939 RAF Coastal Command consisted of eighteen squadrons with 176 aircraft. The quality of the machines was deplorable. Ten squadrons consisted of Avro Ansons. These could carry two 250 lb bombs over a range of up to 600 miles, but their short range made them unsuitable for anything except coastal work. There were also a number of Lockheed Hudsons, which had a longer range – up to 1,900 miles, depending on equipment carried – and could carry up to 1,400 lb of bombs. Hudsons, however, were slow, clumsy and extremely vulnerable when attacked by enemy fighters. The principal weapon carried by these types in the early stages of the war were the standard RAF general-purpose and semi-armour-piecing bombs. These were totally inadequate for use against shipping, frequently bouncing off the target and rolling into the sea. There were also two squadrons of torpedo-bombers, and these used a particularly obsolete type of machine, the Vildebeest, designed as a light bomber in 1926 and totally inadequate for the torpedo-bomber role. The remainder of the Command consisted of a handful of flying-boats. To make matters worse it was decreed that the Ansons and Hudsons should be at the disposal of Bomber Command as well as Coastal Command. The duties assigned to this pathetically under-equipped force were anti-submarine patrols, anti-ship strikes, reconnaissance, minelaying and a host of other chores. The Admiralty was constantly adding to the tasks demanded of the Command, and on several occasions it was suggested that it should be transferred lock, stock, and barrel to navy control, along with the FAA. However, at operational level co-operation between Coastal Command and the naval formations with which it worked was generally good, and by 1941 the two were working together very effectively. In part they were united by their opposition to RAF Bomber Command, which continually fought to retain priority over all other arms in the allocation of production and technical resources.

Unsurprisingly, the performance of Coastal Command in the early stages of the war was unimpressive, but gradually better training, especially in navigation, better equipment and expansion began to have effect. The failure of Operation Rhine Exercise to achieve its objectives is a testament to how professional Coastal Command had become. It was their gallant torpedo attack that had put *Gneisenau* out of action at the critical juncture, and it was their Catalina that found *Bismarck* after she had been lost.

Appendix 3

Bismarck

(See pages 156–157 for diagrams)

Bismarck, when she was launched, was the largest and most effective battleship afloat. She was surpassed in December 1941 when the Japanese *Yamato* (71,600 tons, 18-inch main armament) was completed. Like most German warships, she was of all-welded construction and built according to the principle laid down by the great Admiral Tirpitz, who decreed that the first duty of a battleship was to stay afloat. The whole hull structure was designed with this consideration foremost. Most observers considered her an ugly ship compared to the graceful Italian battleships and the purposeful-looking Japanese super-battle-ships, but her durability showed her to be a triumph of German shipbuilding prowess.

Careful consideration was given to the materials used. Four types of steel were employed for armour plating:

St 52 construction-grade steel.

KC n/A Krupp cementite. This was face-hardened armour plate, designed to absorb terrific impact stress.

Wotan Heart. This was armour plate with a very high tensile strength (85–95 kg/mm^2). It was used for deck armour.

Wotan Weich. This was used for longitudinal torpedo bulkheads.

Vertical protection above the waterline was provided along seventy per cent of the length of the ship by a 16-foot (5.2 m) wide vertical belt 12.5 inches (320 mm) thick. This protected the main decks and the working parts of the ship. It was backed by a 2-inch layer of teak, which was very effective for absorbing shock, and held by through-bolts onto the 1-inch (25 mm) thick side-plating. The object of this was to absorb hits above the waterline. The shell strike from *Prince of Wales* that damaged one of the turbo-generators and the No. 2 boiler-room struck the ship beneath this protective belt and penetrated the torpedo protection below the waterline. It was unfortunate for *Bismarck* that the shell struck below the belt, which would probably have absorbed a hit from a 14-inch projectile with little damage. The protection below the waterline was designed to defend against torpedoes travelling at 30 to 50 kts, not shells travelling at over 1,000 kts.

The practice on British battleships of the period differed from Germans, normally having rather thicker protection near the centre of the ship, and less forward and aft.

Above the main belt the citadel area was protected by 5.75-inch (145 mm) KC plate. This was lighter so as to retain the stability of the hull, but was sufficient to absorb hits from secondary armament. Forward and aft of the main belt 2.3–3.1-inch (60–80 mm) armour was used. To increase protection in the area of the turrets and their magazines, the hull sloped outwards, so that shells would be inclined to hit it at an oblique angle, reducing the possibility of penetration.

Following well-established German practice, great attention was paid to splitting the hull into separate watertight compartments. There were twenty-two watertight bulkheads. The heaviest of these were located at the fore and aft ends of the citadel, and varied from 5.7 inches (145 mm) to 8.6 inches (220 mm) thick. As well as limiting damage by flooding, these protected the citadel from shells coming from ahead or astern, which might penetrate the lighter armour forward or aft of the main belt.

The armoured decking was 2–3.1-inch (50–80 mm) thick Wotan Heart armour, the thickest sections being close to the turrets and the control tower. Below this, protecting vital parts of the ship, was a further horizontal armoured shield, about 3 feet (1 m) above the waterline and sloping down at the edges to join the bottom of the armoured belt just below the water. This was between 4.7 inches (120 mm) and 3.1 inches (80 mm) thick, with the thickest sections around the machinery and magazines. The sloping sides of this shield made it extremely difficult for a shell to penetrate the armoured belt and the shield. The bow and stern of the ship had lighter horizontal protection, but the steering-gear aft had an armoured turtle deck 4.3 inches (120 mm) thick. The fatal torpedo that disabled the ship struck near the rudders well below this.

The shell that cut off oil supply from the forward tanks penetrated the lighter armour in the bow section, forward of the armoured belt.

The turrets were protected by 14.2-inch (360 mm) KC armour on the face, 8.7-inch (220 mm) on the sides and 5.1-inch (130 mm) on top. The forward conning tower had 13.7-inch (350 mm) walls, and the rangefinders and command posts were also heavily armoured. The most exposed position was the foretop command post, high above the bridge, which must have been a very frightening station when in action.

As the story of the ship reveals, the underwater protection from torpedoes and mines was extremely effective. As well as the twenty-two transverse bulkheads and the torpedo bulk-heads, there were longitudinal bulkheads located 18 feet (5.5 m) to 10 feet (3.05 m) inboard of the ship's sides. These were 1.8 inches (45 mm) thick and backed by ductile steel plate. Feedwater for the boilers and fuel oil were stored inboard of the transverse bulkheads, and the outer void between the bulkhead and the armoured belt was used for counter-flooding should the corresponding compartment on the other side of the ship be damaged. The ship had a double bottom, and the space between the two skins was used for storage of liquids and was divided into many small watertight compartments. The failure of several 18-inch torpedoes fired by Swordfish to penetrate the underwater protection is testament to its effectiveness. Even the 21-inch torpedoes fired by surface-ships in the last stages of the battle did not readily cause serious flooding.

Bismarck was driven by an oil-fired, geared, three-shaft, steam turbine system, although other means of propulsion had been considered at the design stage, including diesels and turbo-electric drive. As well as producing the required power, a warship's machinery has to be extremely robust so as to survive battle damage. The machinery was located between bulkheads VII and XIV, quite near the centre of the ship, and it was all below the waterline. As well as the 150,000 hp main engines, there were 7,910 kW of electrical power, partly generated by steam turbo-generators and partly by diesels.

The twelve Wagner Hochdruck high-pressure boilers were distributed in six separate watertight compartments with the turbo-generators just forward of them. It was the port hand turbo-generator, the boiler-room aft of it and adjacent fuel tanks that were damaged by the 14-inch shell from *Prince of Wales* when it struck the torpedo bulkhead beside the generator. Aft of the boilers were two turbines driving the port and starboard propellers, and behind these was the third turbine driving the centre propeller. The position of this turbine and its shaft towards the stern of the ship probably caused it to suffer the shock-related effects of the torpedo that struck and jammed the steering gear. The propellers themselves were 15.4 feet (4.7 m) in diameter. All the turbines were Blohm and Voss sets, with separate low-power units for drive astern. The two diesel generators flanked the aft turbine. They produced 4,000 kW AC power for domestic use and 500 kW DC for the ship's systems. The steam turbo-generators produced 3,910 kW DC. This was all fairly conventional technology, but it was an extremely well-designed and efficient system, which showed itself able to withstand terrible punishment and abuse. The ship carried 8,294 tons of fuel oil at full capacity, giving a range of almost 10,000 nautical miles at 16 kts and 4,500 at 28 kts.

A battleship is essentially a mobile gun platform, and with her high speed, broad beam and effective protective armour *Bismarck* was a particularly formidable one.

The main battery consisted of eight 15-inch guns in four turrets, 'Anton' and 'Bruno' forward, and 'Casar' and 'Dora' aft. The turrets were very large compared with those of other 15-inch eight-gun ships, such as the British battle cruisers, and each was mounted on a roller track giving 145 degrees of traverse on either side. They had a maximum elevation of 30 degrees and depression of 5 degrees. The guns could be elevated and fired independently. These 15-inch guns had an exceptionally high muzzle velocity, giving them a very flat trajectory, which contributed to their excellent accuracy and rapid target acquisition.

A comparison with *King George V*'s main armament is instructive.

	Bismarck	*King George V*
Guns	8 15-inch	10 14-inch
Weight of shot	1,764 lb (800 kg)	1,590 lb (721 kg)
Weight of broadside	14,111 lb (6,401 kg)	15,900 lb (7,210 kg)
Muzzle velocity	2,690 ft/sec (820 m/sec)	2,600 ft/sec (792 m/sec)
Rate of fire	2.4/min	2/min
Range	38,880 yd (35,550 m)	36,300 yd (33,192 m)

Three shell types were used:

Armour-piercing: a very strong shellcase designed to penetrate enemy heavy armour and explode inside vital parts of an enemy ship.

Semi-armour-piercing: containing a larger charge in a less-robust casing for use against more lightly armoured opponents.

High-explosive: for use against merchant ships and shore targets.

1,000 shells would normally be carried.

Fire control was by one of three fire-control stations. The main fire-control station was in the foretop, which was in an exposed position high above the bridge. It was knocked out early in the fight with *Rodney*. Being mounted so high above the waterline it could not be heavily armoured as too much weight aloft would lead to stability problems. The fore and aft directors were lower down in the citadel. The optical rangefinders were in rotating cupolas, with the directors, giving the bearing of the target, just below them. Radar antennae were mounted on the same cupolas. Control of the guns was the responsibility of the gunnery officer, who might at any point delegate control of the fore or aft sets of guns to his assistants in the fore and aft stations. In an emergency any one of the stations could control all the guns, as well as the secondary armament. An indicator in each station told the gunnery officers the readiness state of each of the guns. The guns were fired by pressing a button or blowing into a mouthpiece in the director station. The gunnery officers would carefully watch the fall of shot of each salvo and make any adjustments needed, using a time-of-flight monitor in the computer room to identify each salvo.

To perfect his aim, the gunnery officer would either fire a test shot with one or more guns and observe the splashes carefully, or use a bracketing group to find the target. A bracketing group would consist of three salvos separated by a predetermined range, often 400 metres. Normally one or other of these would straddle the target. The fire-control officer would then know the range and bearing and would call for 'good rapid' fire, adjusting his aim according to the relative movement of the ships. In emergency conditions the turrets could be aimed and fired under local control, but this was seldom accurate enough to be useful. The gunnery officer's job was extremely skilled and required very well developed co-ordination between the various officers and petty officers in the director stations, the computer rooms and the turrets.

The secondary battery consisted of twelve 6-inch guns in three twin two-gun turrets. The projectile weight was 100 lb (45.3 kg) and maximum range 25,150 yards (23,000 m). Their primary purpose was to deter attacking destroyers, as their elevation range of $-10/+40$ degrees made them unsuitable for anti-aircraft work. Rate of fire was 8 rounds/min. These weapons were a weak spot in the design; it would have been better to increase the heavy anti-aircraft battery and used it for both air and sea defence.

The heavy anti-aircraft battery consisted of sixteen 4.1-inch guns in four double mounts. Projectile weight was 33.1 lb (15.1 kg) and maximum range 19,375 yards (17,700 m). Elevation range was −10 or −8/+80 degrees. Rate of fire was 18 rounds/min.

The medium and light anti-aircraft batteries were insufficient for their purpose. They consisted of sixteen 1.5-inch (37 mm) guns in four double mounts, which threw a projectile weighing 1.64 lb (0.745 kg) over a range of 7,383 yards (6,750 m). Elevation range was −10/+80 degrees. Rate of fire was 80 rounds/min. There were also sixteen light (2 cm) flak guns. By contrast *King George V* in 1941 carried five 8-barrelled two-pounder pom-poms, one 4-barrelled two-pounder pom-pom and eighteen 20 mm Oerlikons – a far more powerful AA outfit than *Bismarck*'s. Even this powerful defensive battery was constantly increased as the war went on. *Bismarck*'s light flak guns probably hit attacking Swordfish many times, but failed to bring them down.

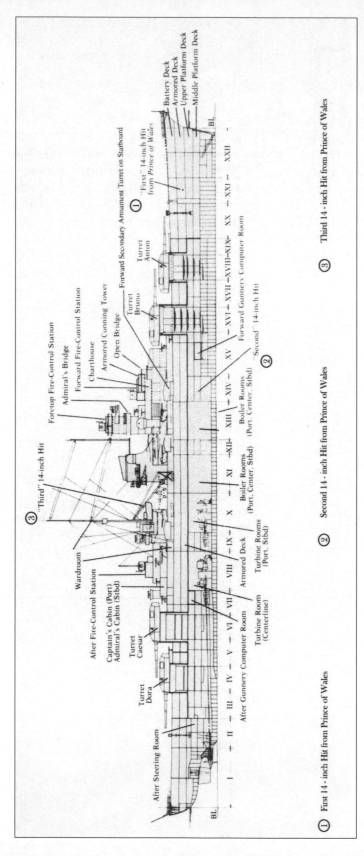

Overall drawing of *Bismarck* showing the watertight compartments and the position of the location of the three shell hits from *Prince of Wales*. Note how the second hit is only just below the waterline and the armoured belt. A foot or so higher and the armoured belt would have stopped it. The first hit was well forward of the belt. Note the rather shallow twin rudders.

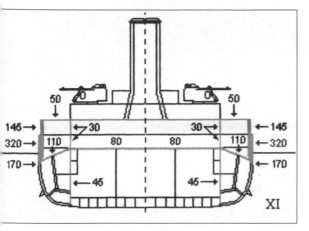

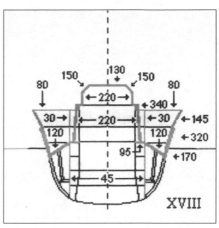

ection through bulkhead XI. The figures indicate thickness of
ne armour in mm. Note the sloping sides of the 80mm thick
rmoured deck joining the underwater section of the hull just
elow the waterline. Also note the 110 mm torpedo bulkhead.
'o damage the ship seriously the blast from an exploding
orpedo would have to penetrate the 170mm underwater hull,
ne torpedo bulkhead and the 45mm longitudinal bulkhead.
'he ship's bottom was remarkably flat and could probably have
een severely damaged by a torpedo fitted with a proximity
use that worked correctly.

Section through bulkhead XVIII. Note the
outward slope of the hull outboard of Anton
turret and the heavily armoured sides of the
turret itself. Note that the effective underwater protection covers this section also.

'lan of the engine rooms between sections VI and XIV. The whole machinery area was below water level and
'lenty of redundancy was provided so as to allow for damage. In practice the engines proved extremely robust
nd reliable in contrast to those of some of the smaller German warships. The engines weighed 2,756 tons and
vere designed to produce 136,000HP. The ship's design speed was 29 knots, but in fact she achieved almost 31,
ne engines producing well over their designed power output.

	Port Electric Plant No. 2		Port Turbine Room	Port No. 1 Boiler Room Boiler No. 1529 Boiler No. 1532		Port No. 2 Boiler Room Boiler No. 1535 Boiler No. 1538	Port Electric Plant No. 4
	Centre Turbine Room			Centre No. 1 Boiler Room Boiler No. 1530 Boiler No. 1533		Centre No. 2 Boiler Room Boiler No. 1536 Boiler No. 1539	
Diesel Motor Room No.1	Starboard Electric Plant No. 1		Starboard Turbine Room	Starboard No. 1 Boiler Room Boiler No. 1531 Boiler No. 1534		Starboard No. 2 Boiler Room Boiler No 1537 Boiler No. 1540	Starboard Electric Plant No. 3

| VII | VIII | IX | X | XI | XII | XIII | XIV |

- Boilers
- Turbines
- Turbo Generators
- Auxiliary Machinery
- Diesel Generators
- Fuel Bunkers

APPENDIX 4

The Naval Treaties

The Treaty of Versailles in 1919 deprived Germany of her navy, most of which was famously scuttled at Scapa Flow.

The treaty was repudiated by the USA, which for political reasons preferred a programme of general naval disarmament that was to be binding on all nations, and left the USA and the UK as the two major naval powers of the world. Americans were already worried by Japanese naval expansion in the Pacific. This led to the most important of the arms limitation treaties, the Washington Agreement, which was an entirely naval arms limitation treaty and was signed on 6 February 1921. This allowed Britain and the USA 580,450 tons of warships each, Japan 301,320 tons, France 221,170 tons and Italy 182,800 tons. This was to be reduced to 500,000 for the USA and Britain, 300,000 for Japan and 175,000 for France and Italy when the planned post-war scrapping of obsolete ships was complete. The maximum tonnage of any warship was to be 35,000 tons and maximum gun size 16-inch.

No new construction of capital ships was to be allowed for ten years.

Aircraft carriers were deemed to be special ships and were allocated on the basis of equality for Britain and the USA, again to be followed by Japan, with France and Italy having the smallest allocations. Size was limited to 33,000 tons. Cruisers were limited to 10,000 tons and 8-inch main armament, and destroyers to 1,500 tons (2,000 for destroyer leaders).

Both Britain and the USA were obliged to scrap many of their older battleships and battle cruisers, a cause of much bitterness in naval circles at the time, although in fact few of the ships scrapped would have been of much value in any subsequent conflict.

Some exceptions to treaty obligations as regards new warship building were made for ships already laid down, including *Nelson* and *Rodney*, and some half-built Japanese and US battleships that were converted into aircraft carriers.

Numerous subsequent disarmament conferences and naval treaties effecting warship building were completed during the inter-war period. The Geneva Treaty of 1927 endeavoured to define more closely the limitations on cruiser armament and size, and to outlaw a new generation of heavily armed 'cruiser submarines'. It had been convened with quite ambitious objectives, but lack of agreement between the powers involved, especially Japan and the USA, limited the level of agreement achieved. The First London Agreement of 1930 was concluded between the USA, Britain and Japan. In it the concept of 'taking risks for peace' was first embodied, the risks being entirely on the side of the democracies. Essentially this agreement obliged the USA and Britain to scrap some further obsolete battleships, and allowed Japan to increase its navy from sixty per cent to roughly eighty per cent of US total tonnage. In reality this treaty did almost nothing to mollify the Japanese feeling of injustice to which Washington had given rise.

The Anglo-German Naval Agreement (AGNA) of 1936 was entirely an Anglo-German affair. It effectively nullified the Versailles Treaty, as it allowed Germany to build a navy thirty-five per cent as large as that of Britain. Within this overall tonnage limit, Germany could build as many submarines as it liked subject to some formal approvals. This agreement was much resented by France and Italy, as they were not consulted. The British, however, had always considered the terms of Versailles too harsh for the Germans to tolerate in the long term. When Hitler first came to power he was hoping to woo Britain away from France, and felt that a bi-lateral naval treaty with Britain on terms that Britain might believe reasonable would be a means of achieving this. Britain jumped at the bait.

159

In reality Germany never got anywhere near the thirty-five per cent limit, but this was because war broke out before she had time to construct the ships planned. However, as we have seen, many of her warships were far outside the limits imposed by Washington.

By the late 1930s Hitler had lost confidence in Britain as a potential ally, and authorised the implementation of 'Plan Z'. At the launch party for *Tirpitz* in March 1939 he publicly denounced the AGNA. Plan Z would of course give Germany a far bigger navy than the AGNA allowed. For a brief period naval construction was given a green light in Germany, and had priority access to skilled labour and materials.

Altogether the various disarmament agreements and naval agreements were no more than a useless sham, as the potential aggressor nations, Germany, Italy and Japan, initially tried to circumvent them by stealth, and then became sufficiently confident to ignore them altogether, while the democracies, especially Britain, observed them to the letter. There was no system of verification in the treaties, they depended on the good will of the signatories, and there were no sanctions whatever for transgressions. They were superbly successful in satisfying the pacifist principles fashionable in the democracies and in supporting British and American finance ministries in their drive to reduce the naval estimates. At the same time they gave fatal encouragement to those who sought to gain from a second world war.

Main Events in the Voyage of *Bismarck*

	Date	Time
Bismarck commissioned	24-Aug-40	
Bismarck and *Prinz Eugen* leave Gotenhafen	18-May-41	21.30 hrs
Spotted by *Gotland*	20-May-41	15.00 hrs
Reported by Norwegian Intelligence	20 May-41	19.00 hrs
Enter fjord	21-May-41	10.00 hrs
Confirmed by photo-reconnaissance Spitfire	21-May-41	13.15 hrs
Bismarck and *Prinz Eugen* leave fjord	21-May-41	19.30 hrs
Hood and *Prince of Wales* put to sea	22-May-41	00.15 hrs
Fjord reported empty by *Maryland*	22-May-41	19.40 hrs
King George V and *Victorious* put to sea	22-May-41	22.15 hrs
Hitler suggests to Raeder operation called off	22-May-41	23.00 hrs
Suffolk detects *Bismarck*	23-May-41	19.15 hrs
Suffolk loses contact	24-May-41	00.28 hrs
Hood and *Prince of Wales* pass close to *Bismarck*	24-May-41	01.30 hrs
Force H puts to sea	23-May-41	02.00 hrs
Suffolk regains contact	24-May-41	03.00 hrs
Hood and *Prince of Wales* open fire	24-May-41	05.53 hrs

	Date	Time
Hood blows up	24-May-41	05.56 hrs
Prince of Wales turns away	24-May-41	06.03 hrs
Lutjens informs HQ that he intends to make for French port	24-May-41	07.00 hrs
Prinz Eugen departs	24-May-41	18.00 hrs
Attack by *Victorious*'s aircraft	25-May-41	00.01 hrs
Suffolk loses contact	25-May-41	03.30 hrs
Lutjens sends two signals	25-May-41	09.00 hrs
Tovey steers north-east	25-May-41	10.47 hrs
Tovey turns south-east	25-May-41	18.00 hrs
Catalina makes sighting	26-May-41	10.30 hrs
Swordfish from *Ark Royal* makes sighting	26-May-41	11.00 hrs
Attack misdirected to *Sheffield*	26-May-41	16.00 hrs
Rodney joins Tovey	26-May-41	18.00 hrs
Successful attack by Swordfish	26-May-41	20.30 hrs
Attack by destroyers	26-May-41	23.00 hrs
Norfolk makes contact	27-May-41	08.30 hrs
Rodney opens fire	27-May-41	09.02 hrs
Bismarck sinks	27-May-41	10.40 hrs

Index